TRACING YOUR
SCOTTISH
ANCESTORS

FAMILY HISTORY FROM PEN & SWORD BOOKS

Tracing Your Yorkshire Ancestors
Rachel Bellerby

Tracing Your Royal Marine Ancestors
Richard Brooks and Matthew Little

Tracing Your Army Ancestors
Simon Fowler

A Guide to Military History on the Internet
Simon Fowler

Tracing Your Northern Ancestors
Keith Gregson

Your Irish Ancestors
Ian Maxwell

Tracing Your Air Force Ancestors
Phil Tomaselli

Tracing Your Jewish Ancestors
Rosemary Wenzerul

TRACING YOUR
SCOTTISH ANCESTORS

A GUIDE FOR
FAMILY HISTORIANS

Ian Maxwell

Scotland is indefinable it has no unity except upon the map. Two languages, many dialects, innumerable forms of piety, and countless local patriotisms and prejudices, part us among ourselves...

R.L. Stevenson

Pen & Sword
FAMILY HISTORY

Dedication

To my father who inspired in me a love of the old country

First published in Great Britain in 2009 by

PEN AND SWORD FAMILY HISTORY

an imprint of
Pen & Sword Books Ltd
47 Church Street
Barnsley
South Yorkshire
S70 2AS

Copyright © Ian Maxwell 2009

ISBN 978 1 84415 9918

A CIP catalogue record for this book is
available from the British Library

Typeset in 10pt Palatino by Mac Style, Beverley, East Yorkshire
Printed and bound in the UK by CPI

Pen & Sword Books Ltd incorporates the Imprints of Pen & Sword
Aviation, Pen & Sword Maritime, Pen & Sword Military,
Wharncliffe Local History, Pen and Sword Select, Pen and Sword
Military Classics, Leo Cooper, Remember When, Seaforth Publishing
and Frontline Publishing.

For a complete list of Pen & Sword titles please contact
PEN & SWORD BOOKS LIMITED
47 Church Street, Barnsley, South Yorkshire, S70 2AS, England
E-mail: enquiries@pen-and-sword.co.uk
Website: www.pen-and-sword.co.uk

CONTENTS

ABBREVIATIONS

NAS   National Archives Scotland
NLS   National Library Scotland
OPRs Old Parish Registers
GROS General Registry Office Scotland
OSA   Old Statistical Account
NRA   National Register of Archives
SCAN Scottish Archive Network
TNA   The National Archives (London)
NSA   New Statistical Account

Great Hall, Parliament House. From James Grant, Old & New Edinburgh, *issued in weekly instalments c.1890.*

INTRODUCTION

Scotland's history had been influenced by many factors: the division of the country by its language, with its Gaelic-speaking population in the Highlands and its anglicized population in the Lowlands; the Reformation which impacted most dramatically in the Lowlands, with many of the Highland clans remaining local to the old church; and, of course, its geography with successive ways of invaders and settlers gravitating to the more fertile arable regions of the Lowlands rather than the comparatively barren Highlands.

These physical factors had their effects on the earliest known settlers in Scotland. The majority of the Bronze and early Iron Age settlements for example are to be found along the east coast in the Lowlands. The Romans penetrated as far as Aberdeenshire but they built their northermost defences, the Antonie Wall, along the line of the Forth and Clyde valleys on the edge of the central Lowlands. South of the Forth-Clyde there were several British tribes, recorded by the Romans: the Selgovae, Novantae, Damnonii and Votadini. By the sixth century these had developed into the British kingdom of Strathclyde and Rheged, in south-west Scotland, and Gododdin in Lothian.

The best known inhabitants of Scotland by the fifth century AD were the Picts. They lived in the central and eastern parts of the country. To the sixth century cleric Gildas, the Picts were 'a foul horde'. They remain a mystery to this day, leaving only strange symbols carved on standing stones and place names such as at Pitlochry or Pitmadden. Pictish place-names can be recognised by the words pert (wood) caer (fort) pren (tree) aber (river mouth) and a few others. The Picts spoke a form of Celtic like the British and Welsh though different from their Scotti neighbours so that St Columba when he arrived from Ireland needed an interpreter to speak to them.

In the sixth century the Scotti, also known as the Dal Riata, invaded from the north of Ireland and settled in the western region known as Argyll. They introduced their own names, such as achadh (field or settlement) sliabh (mountain) baile (settlement) and most distinctive of all cill (church) usually

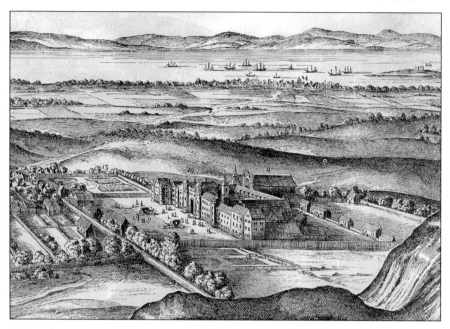

Holyrood Palace and Abbey. From James Grant, Old & New Edinburgh, *issued in weekly instalments c.1890.*

combined with a saint's name. Of course, it was this Irish tribe who gave us the name Scotland. Gildas, writing in the sixth century AD, declared: 'As the Romans went back home, there eagerly emerged from the coracles that had carried them across the sea valleys the foul hordes of Scots and Picts, like dark throngs of worms who wriggle out of narrow fissures in the rock … they were readier to cover their villainous faces with hair than their private parts … with clothes'.

The Celts were followed by the Angles, who settled in south-eastern Scotland. They were in turn followed by the Norsemen from Scandinavia, who raided both the east and west coasts indiscriminately. Although they settled along the west coast and as far south as the Moray Firth on the east coast, it was principally in the Orkney and Shetland Islands, and in Caithness that they settled permanently. These places remained under Norwegian sovereignty for centuries after the rest of Scotland was united under one king.

In 844 the Picts and the Scots were unified under the rule of Kenneth MacAlpin forming a united Scotland north of the Forth and Clyde valleys. In 1018 under Malcolm II, the Scots defeated the Angles at Carham on the Tweed and conquered the land of Lothian. In the same year Malcolm also inherited the kingdom of Strathclyde, or Cumbria. With the gradual anglicizing of the southern area, it was not perhaps surprising that the more aggressive Teutonic peoples gradually drove the Celtcs into the mountainous regions of the Highlands.

During the twelfth and thirteenth centuries there was one further mixture to the many stains that finally made up the Scottish race, caused by the arrival of various Norman adventurers and their followers to take up high office in church and state. Under David I huge estates in southern Scotland were dispensed to Normans: Renfrewshire went to Walter FitzAlan, who in Scotland took the name 'Steward' from the office he and his family held at the Royal court. By the fourteenth century Walter's descendants were calling themselves the 'Stuarts' and would rule Scotland and eventually England until the early eighteenth century. Another incomer was Robert de Brus, Lord of Brix in the Cotentin peninsula of Normany and of Cleveland in Yorkshire. It was under a de Brus, of course, that the Scottish nation was utimately united in the fourteenth century.

The story was very different in the Islands (the Hebrides and the Orkneys and Shetlands). Under Norwegian rule for hundreds of years, the Hebrides returned to Scottish sovereignty in the thirteenth century, but the Orkneys and Shetlands only came back under Scottish rule in the fifteenth century. Therefore their language, names and entire way of life resembled the Norwegian more closely than the Scottish. This changed during the later half of the sixteenth century when there was a considerable movement of Lowland Scots into Shetland. The introduction of Scottish bishops to Orkney throughout the previous century and a half had resulted in large numbers of Scots accompanying them as dependents. By the mid-sixteenth century, accordingly, the Norse language had begun to disappear in Orkney, being replaced by Lowland Scots. By the start of the seventeenth century the same process was almost complete in Shetland, though the Isles inevitably retained marks of their long period of Norwegian rule.

The early history of Scotland is therefore both rich and complex, and it is a common heritage shared by those of with Scottish ancestors who now inhabitant every corner of the globe. Although Scotland is a small country with less than five million inhabitants, there are reckoned to be thirty

Tobermory, on the Isle of Mull. From William Daniell, Voyage Round Great Britain, *1820.*

million persons of Scottish decent scattered across the world. For both those who remain in Scotland, and those of Scottish descent who have had such a impact both south of the border, in Ireland and in the USA, Canada, Australia and New Zealand, there is a common bond: a distinctively Scottish surname.

Surnames began to be used in Scotland from the twelfth century, and became common in the fourteenth. During the twelfth century some families of French or English extraction, who already had hereditary surnames, became major landowners in the country. These included families such as Bruce, Balliol, Fraser, Graham and Stuart. The spread of recognisably surnames in Scotland, nevertheless, appears to have been slow. As late as the fourteenth century the surnames used by the majority in the Lowlands of Scotland do not appear to have been substantially different in their general character from those employed in England at the same time.

Surnames from personal names with the addition of '-son' occur from the thirteenth century onwards. It is therefore not surprising to find that Scotland has a high quota of patronymics and the Lowland names

Scenes at Edinburgh Castle. The Graphic, 1882

Thomson, Robertson, Wilson, Anderson, Paterson, Watson and Henderson are among the thirty commonest. Some of these had Gaelic personal name as the first element, such as Finlayson or Malcolmson, and these may be Anglicised forms of Gaelic names which began with the prefix- 'Mac'.

The general spread of hereditary surnames in the Lowlands was not complete until the sixteenth century. There were many cases where tenants or other dependents of major landowners assumed their overlords' surnames as their own. This is believed to have happened on a large scale with the surname Gordon in the fifteenth century explaining why the name became was common in the north-east of Scotland at this time. The surnames Douglas, common in the Borders and south-west, and Stewart common in several areas are also examples of the process whereby tenants assumed the name of their masters.

Most late-medieval trades are commemorated in occupational names, and those with a peculiarly Scottish accent include Lamont (law-man), Lorimer (harness-maker), Naismith (cutler), Napier (linen-draper) and Sillars (silversmith). Various types of herdsmen are recorded in Hoggarth, Shephed and Stoddart. Another occupational surname, Smith is the commonest name in Scotland. The great prevalence of certain leading surnames in various towns and villages in Scotland led to the introduction of an organized system of distinctive nicknames. Brown (the second commonest name in Scotland), Black, Gray, White, Small and Young are common to both Scotland and England. One of the most celebrated of Highland names – Campbell- belongs to the nickname class, as do Forsyth and Kennedy.

Another type of nickname is racial in character. Scott is perhaps the most famous of these names; it dates from the time when non-Scottish inhabitants of North Britain (in the form of Britons, Angles and Normans) were still clearly identifiable; and ethnic diversity is further illustrated by the names Wallace, Galbraith and Inglis. In 'Notes and Queries', 22 May 1915, Sir Herbert Maxwell, draws attention to an article in *Blackwood's Magazine*, March 1842, on the subject of these 'tee-names', as they are sometimes called:

> It seems that there were then in the little seaport of Buckie no fewer than twenty-five males rejoicing in the name of George Cowie, distinguished from each other as Carrot, Doodle, Neep, Biglugs, Beauty, Bam, Helldom, Collop, Stoattie, Snuffers, Rochie, Toothie, Todlowrie, &c.

When surnames came to be adopted in the Highlands, the form Mac, meaning 'son of' was added to the original name. Thus the son of Donald became MacDonald. It is not surprising in view of the considerable Scandinavian settlement in parts of Scotland that the second element is a Scandinavian person name such as MacManus, MacIver and MacLeod. Although outsiders now most closely identify surnames beginning with Mac with Scotland, they account for no more than twenty per cent of Scotland's surnames, even in the Highlands.

Heriditary surnames have a separate history in the Gaelic-speaking parts of Scotland. As long as the clan system survived until well into the eighteenth century, surnames were those of the clans rather than individual familes. When the territory inhabited by a clan expanded, often through warfare, the inhabitants of those parts would generally assume the name of this clan. There is no evidence to suppose that all members of a clan were descended from a common ancestor. It was only by the middle of the eighteenth century that clan names were gradually transformed into hereditary surnames. But its was only with compulsory registration of births deaths and marriages in Scotland, which began in 1855 that registrars started to insist that individuals should use the same surname as their father.

Until well into the eighteenth century, names from the Gaelic-speaking regions were not very common in other parts of Scotland. Increasingly migration to the Lowlands in search of work, resulted in the increasing appearance of Gaelic names south of the Tay, although these were often drastically changed by being Anglicised in various ways. In some cases patronymics were changed into surnames ending in '-son' so that, for instance, MacDonald became Donaldson.

Surnames at first were shifting things, and it took several generations for a name to become established within a family. Even then, it could change. When the surname of the MacGregors was forbidden by law for most of the seventeenth century, they became Campbells, or Comries, or Whites. Some changed back, others did not.

Although the development of hereditary surnames in Scotland began later that it did in England or Ireland, the distinctiveness of those surnames and there association with particular parts of the country has been a great asset to those tracing their Scottish roots. It is clear that the development of surnames in Scotland is highy reflective of both its history and social structure. This book aims to take a closer look at the social history of Scotland and show what records can be used to discover that elusive Scottish ancestor.

Chapter One

THE LIVES OF OUR ANCESTORS

Birth, death and marriage

Funerals, the Kirk insisted, were not occasions for dancing and merrymaking. In 1755 an Act was passed which forbade 'promiscuous dancing at burials and other occasions' and numerous addresses and pamphlets followed. Scotland was a poor country and the Kirk objected to the money spent on funerals, marriages and baptisms and to the wide range of superstitions and pre-Reformation practices which generally accompanied such family occasions. Neither did local ministers take kindly to the lavish quantities of drink provided for guests often over a period of several days. In the case of the mother of Duncan Forbes of Culloden the party arrived at the grave only to discover that the corpse had been left behind. At the Laird of Abbotsburgh's burial the company appeared so rosy and merry in the kirkyard, that some English dragoons quartered at Falkirk said to one another: 'Jolly dogs! A Scots burial is merrier than our weddings.'

Prior to the introduction of civil registration in Scotland on 1 January 1855, records of births and baptisms, deaths and burials and proclamations and marriages were kept by the Church. In 1551 the Provincial Council of the Scottish Clergy enacted that a register of baptisms and marriages be kept. However, in 1588 the General Assembly of the Church of Scotland complained that 'there is neither religion nor discipline with the poor, but the most part live in fifthly adultery, incest, fornication, their barnes unbaptized, and themselves never resort to the Kirk, nor participate [in] the sacraments'.

Baptisms, burials and banns of marriage were supposed to be entered in registers kept by every parish Kirk session (a governing body of elders nominated by the congregation and chaired by the parish minister), but the quality and regularity of these volumes varied greatly, and they were not always carefully preserved. In fact, only 99 of the 850 parishes that returned information for the 1801 census possessed regular registers. The remainder either kept no register at all, or made only sporadic entries.

The imperfect condition of Scottish parish registers attracted the attention of various writers as early as the latter part of the eighteenth century. Hugo Arnot, in his *History of Edinburgh*, published in the year 1779, makes the following observations respecting the registers of the metropolis:

> As to the registers of births and burials in Edinburgh, they have of late been kept in such a manner as to render them, (if any arguments be drawn from them,) the infallible sources of error. The register of burials is kept by people whose faculties are impaired by drinking, who forget to-day what was done yesterday: people who have an interest in reducing the list of burials, as thereby they may peculate the share of the mortcloth (or pall) money due to the charity workhouse. Besides, they enter not into the list of burials any who have died without receiving baptism; nor those whose relations are so poor as not to be able to pay for the use of a mortcloth; nor those who die in the charity workhouse.

Those registers which were kept with any degree of accuracy did not always survive. Some were lost or destroyed, while others were borrowed, usually for legal purposes and were never returned. In numerous instances they have been burnt, along with the manse or school-house, in which they happened to be deposited ; and one unfortunate record appears to have met with a watery grave, having been dropped by the person to whom it was entrusted, while he was ' in the act of crossing a rapid stream !'

The inaccuracy of those records that did survive where highlighted in various court cases in the nineteenth century. At a court case in 1825, the central point at issue was whether a Mrs Catherine Fraser, or Koberton, survived the second day of July 1802. The presiding judge observed, 'It is clear that this woman died in a month of October, and the only question is, whether it was in October 1801, or 1802 ? It is much to be regretted,' he added 'that there is no register of births, deaths, and marriages, as the want of it may, in this case, be productive of injustice to one or other of the parties, and much benefit arises from their being regularly kept.'

Calton Burial Ground, Hume's grave. From James Grant, Old & New Edinburgh, *issued in weekly instalments c.1890.*

To make matters worse, the fees demanded by the kirk session clerks for their trouble in recording events such as births deterred poorer parishioners from coming forward, and since the registers belonged to the Church of Scotland, people of other denominations frequently refused to report births, deaths or marriages on principle. The reluctance on the part of the Dissenters to take advantage of the benefits of registration, is specially referred to in the accounts of various parishes. According to the minister of Kirkconnell, Dumfries, the children of Dissenters are not included in the parochial records, as the parents decline to make any use of these, 'either to avoid paying the usual small perquisite to the clerk, or, as is supposed by most people, because it is a part of their political etiquette, to express in this way their dread of contagion, or contamination, from even a parochial record.'

Even when no fee was charged, as in the parish of Kirkpatrick-Durham in Kirkcudbrightshire, the minister lamented that 'unless I ascertain a child's birth when I baptize it, the parents never think it worth their while to give me a note of it.' This meant that many individuals possessed no record of their birth or parentage to prove an inheritance claim, while medical men, statisticians and municipal authorities found it impossible to ascertain the true number of births, deaths and marriages in any parish. With so many failing to register important events, the family Bible became a vital record for future generations. According to John Firth, writing about Orkney in the 1920s:

> Prior to the passing of the Registration Act, 1855, the only record of births was the list of baptisms kept by the minister, and very often when changes came in the ministry those records were lost. It was, however, customary to have a list of names of a family, with their dates of birth, written out in the big Family Bible, and if this were omitted there were seldom any other means by which ages could be ascertained. In passing, may be mentioned that in the absence of any other available data the Family Bible is frequently used by the Pension Officer when determining whether or not the applicant has reached the age to qualify him or her for an Old Age Pension.

By the early nineteenth century there was increasing public agitation that a compulsory system of civil registration in Scotland was necessary – a demand that got stronger after England's compulsory registration Act in 1837. Among the most prominent advocates of similar legislation for Scotland was the Royal College of Physicians of Edinburgh. The College Fellows stressed the desirability of recording births rather than baptisms; deaths as opposed to burials; and marriages rather than proclamations of banns, as couples who announced their intention to marry did not always proceed with the wedding. Above all, they were 'desirous to see tables of the deaths taking place throughout the Country recorded with regularity and correctness, [so] that they might be useful in illustrating the nature and effects of epidemics, the mortality from different diseases, and prevalence of particular diseases in certain localities, the mortality at different periods of life, the comparative salubrity of Town and Country districts, and all those questions in vital statistics, which may enable the Physicians to understand the causes of diseases epidemic, endemic and sporadic, and to adopt the means most likely to prevent diseases susceptible of prevention, to diminish mortality, to improve health, and to extend if practicable, the average duration of human life'. The Aberdeen Society of Advocates complained of

Isobel Taylor, aged 105. From John Kay, A Series of Original Portraits, With Biographical Sketches and Illustrative Anecdotes. *A C Black: Edinburgh, 1877*

ISOBEL TAYLOR Aged 105 widow of JOHN ALICE
She was Born in the parish of Crieff County of Perth the 4 of March 1713.
and died in Edin' the 23 of April 1818.

'great difficulties in tracing pedigrees and otherwise ascertaining questions of succession to both real and personal estates, in consequence of the Registers...not having hitherto been kept on a complete, regular and uniform plan'.

Between 1829 and 1854, no fewer than nine Scottish registration bills were brought into parliament. The first eight were all rejected, postponed or withdrawn owing to disagreements over who should serve as the new civil registrars, fears of high cost to the taxpayer and excessive administrative machinery, and, most importantly, indignation that four of the bills were accompanied by measures for amending the Scots law of marriage. Scottish lawyers, clergymen and ordinary people were so resistant to any change in the marriage law that they effectively rejected the registration bills by association. The ninth bill, framed by Lord Elcho and passed in 1854, succeeded because it kept administrative costs as low as possible, placated the Church of Scotland by appointing its session clerks as registrars, and did not attempt to interfere with the marriage law.

Registration of births, marriages and deaths began in Scotland on 1 January 1855. The civil section of that Code moved responsibility for registration from the Church to the State. The Act provided for the setting up of the General Registry Office, the appointment of the Register General and his staff to administer the registration system and the appointment by local authorities of a registrar in every parish. In order that registration should be compulsory, penalties were prescribed for parties who failed to register births or deaths and for medical attendants who failed to transmit death certificates to the registrar. The new Act did not require informants to pay any fees for registering a birth or death, unless the former were registered beyond the statutory period of three months, or for registering a marriage, unless the couple requested the registrar to attend the ceremony for this purpose.

Despite their reluctance to register with the authorities, contemporary accounts underline the importance that Scots placed upon the great family events. The significance of such occasions in rural Scotland can be judged by the complex mythology that surrounded them. Baptisms, when the important soul of the child was at stake, attracted a wide range of superstitions despite repeated attempts by the Kirk to stamp them out. Alexander Polson, in the *Folklore of Caithness*, published 1907, recalled 'It is considered especially unlucky that [a child] should be baptized in another year than that in which it was born – hence the great number of baptisms annually taking place during the last weeks of December.'

Baptismal practices underlined the importance of kinship and family ties to Scots across the country. The Rev John Lane Buchanan, in *Travels in the Western Hebrides*, 1782–90, wrote:

> Their baptisms are accompanied with ceremonies that are innocent and useful, for cementing the peace of the country, more especially among themselves. Baptism is administered either in public or in private; – just as it suits the conveniency of themselves and their minister. After this the parents present the child to some neighbour, and call him gosti, or god-father; and after kissing and blessing the child, the gosti delivers the infant to the mother, and ever afterwards looks upon himself as bound not only to be careful of that infant, but also very much attached to the parents. They call one another gosties during life. This name becomes more familiar to them than their own Christian names. Nay, if they had formerly been at variance, by this simple union they become reconciled to one another. They never come to the minister, without a bottle of spirits, and are commonly merry on the occasion.

Many of the baptismal practices were steeped in pre-Christian superstition which survived the Reformation and the strict Presbyterian outlook of the majority of the population. It was essential that the baby was baptised at the earliest possible date as the Rev Walter Gregor, from Echo, wrote towards the end of the nineteenth century: 'Baptism was administered as early as circumstances would permit, and for various reasons. Without this sacrament the child was peculiarly exposed to the danger of being carried off or changed by the fairies. It could not be taken out of the house, at least to any great distance, or into a neighbour's, till it was baptised.' A particularly prohibition surrounded the naming of a child. The Rev Gregor recalled:

> It could not be called by its name till after it was baptised. It was unlawful to pronounce the name, and no one would have dared to ask it. At the baptism the name was commonly written on a slip of paper, which was handed to the minister. Death might come and take away the young one, and if not baptised its name could not be written in the 'Book of Life', and Heaven was closed against it.

Edinburgh General Lying-in Hospital. Lothian Health Services' Archive

Many a mother has been made unhappy by the death of her baby without baptism; and, if the child fell ill, there was no delay in sending for the minister to administer the holy rite, even although at a late hour at night. It was a common belief that in such cases the minister either 'killed or cured'. There was an undefinable sort of awe about unbaptised infants, as well as an idea of uncanniness in having them without baptism in the house.

A great many superstitions surrounded the baptismal ceremony which must have dismayed the conscientious cleric. Alexander MacDonald, *Song and Story from Loch Ness-side*, wrote of Inverness-shire, 1914:

> The hoary-headed spectre, superstition, played its part in connection with the function in many ways. If a word of the baptism service was lost – not distinctly spoken by the minister – the child would grow up to be a somnambulist; if a girl and boy were being baptised at the same time, and that the respective names were by mistake transposed, the former would have a man's beard, and the latter a woman's bare face.

Marriage too was accompanied by a wide range of practices and superstitions. It was a common practise throughout Scotland until well into the eighteenth century on the eve of the wedding for the young friends of the bride and bridegroom to meet at their respective houses for the ceremony of feet-washing. This particular ritual often started with the bride's attendants borrowing the wedding ring and throwing it into a pail of water. The girls scrambled for it, and the lucky winner was acclaimed as the one likely to be the next to marry.

Weddings were above all boisterous occasions accompanied by a great deal of drinking and, as the Kirk complained, 'promiscuous dancing of men and women'. This was equally true of the sumptuous weddings of the rich which led many a laird into debt, and of the 'Penny Bridals' of the poor for which each neighbour contributed a few pennies or brought enough food and drink to make a modest feast. Captain Edward Burt, stationed at Inverness, in 1726 describes one such scene in the Highlands:

> The bride must go about the room, and kiss every man in the company, and in the end every body puts money into a dish,

according to their inclination and ability. By this means, a family in good circumstance, and respected by those they invite, have procured for the new couple wherewithal to begin the world pretty comfortably for people of their low condition … the whole expense of the feast and fiddlers is paid out of the contributions. This and the former are likewise customs all over the Lowlands of Scotland … the do not use the ring in marriage as in England.

One very common superstition surrounded the belief that it was unlucky to marry in the month of May. The Rev James Napier, wrote in 1879, 'One very prevalent superstition, common alike to all classes in the community, and whose force is still not yet spent, was the belief that it was unlucky to marry in the month of May. The aversion to marrying in May finds expression in the very ancient and well-known proverb, 'marry in May, rue for aye', and thousands still avoid marrying in this month who can render no more sold reason for their aversion than the authority of this old proverb … Superstitions of this sort linger much longer in the country than in towns, and the larger the town the more speedily do they die out; but, judging from the statistics of late years, this superstition has still a firm hold of the inhabitants of Glasgow, the second city of the Empire.' Marriage statistics in Scotland from 1810 to 1990 reveal that there is a marked down-swing from April to May, and then a dramatic up-swing in June of each decade.

Until 1929 (when the minimum age was raised to 16), boys could marry at 14 and girls at 12 provided they had parental consent. A 'regular' marriage was one for which the banns were publicly proclaimed in the parish churches of both parties by a minister of religion in the presence of at least two witnesses. The marriage could take place in any building, not just a church, and marriage certificates show that the wedding often took place in a public building, such as a hotel or hall, at the manse or in the home of the bride. Originally the officiating clergyman had to be the parish minister but under the Toleration Act of 1712 an Epicopalian clergyman could officiate. The Marriage (Scotland) Act of 1834 allowed other dissenting ministers, including Roman Catholic priests, to celebrate marriage as long as the banns were proclaimed in the parish church.

There were also several kinds of 'irregular marriages' which were also legal. A clandestine marriage, known as an 'inorderly marriage' was one celebrated by a minister of religion of some congregation but without the preceding publication of the banns. Neither the consent of parents nor the presence of witnesses were required. A marriage could also be established by the statement of consent of both parties or by a promise of marriage in the future followed by sexual intercourse. Because such things happened in private, various types of evidence came to be accepted in disputed marriage cases, such as letters in which the man wrote, or referred, to the women as his wife, or the fact that the couple cohabited and were considered by their neighbours and relations to be husband and wife.

The difficulty arose when one party claimed to be married and the other denied this. The national consistory court (Edinburgh Commissary Court) was the only one in Scotland that could determine whether a legal marriage existed, though litigants could appeal to the higher civil court, the Court of Session and from there to the House of Lords. The process was termed a 'Declarator of Marriage'. The case of Captain John Campbell of Carrick who died at the battle of Fontenoy in 1746 is just one example of the difficulties a widow faced in proving a legitimate marriage. Although Captain Campbell had been living with Jean Campbell as his wife for some twenty years, Magdalen Cochran claimed a pension as the Captain's widow. Jean Campbell had responded by starting a Declarator of Marriage process before the Commissary Court. She had married Captain Campbell irregularly on 9 December 1725 in Roseneath, Dunbartonshire and was able to produce a certificate of the marriage as well as an extract from the minutes of the kirk session of Roseneath revealing that John Campell had acknowledged his irregular marriage to Jean and promised to adhere to her.

Magdalen Cochran, on the other hand, claimed to had been irregularly married to John Campbell at the Abbey of Paisley on 3 July 1724. She did not have a certificate of this marriage but did have a later document signed by Campbell acknowledging the marriage. Having lost the case in the Commissary Court and failed to overturn this ruling in the Court of Session, she appealed to the House of Lords. In January 1753 the House of Lords upheld the commissaries' decision, but called for new legislation to prevent clandestine marriages. Although the Hardwicke Act became law in England in 1754, which required both parties to a marriage below the age of 21 required the consent of their parents, it did not apply in Scotland. Many elopers therefore travelled from south of the border to the first Scottish village they encountered, Gretna Green, to be married.

After the introduction of statutory registration in 1855, some of those who entered into irregular marriages wanted legal evidence of their marriage

Penny Wedding. From Henry Grey Graham, The Social Life of Scotland in the Eighteenth Century. Adam & Charles Black, 1901

and such persons were able to apply to the sheriff of the county within three months of their marriage for a warrant to register such a marriage, which was then entered in the statutory registers. However, many irregular marriages were not recorded by the registrars for the rest of the nineteenth century.

It is hardly surprising, given the fight for survival many in Scotland faced throughout their lives, that any travel writers during the eighteenth and nineteenth century commented that the Scottish placed great emphasis on the manner of their send-off. The Rev Walter Gregor, noted in *Folk Lore: or, Superstitious Beliefs in the West of Scotland within this Century* (Paisley, 1879):

> The body was sedulously watched day and night, more particularly, however, during night. The watching during the night was called the lyke or the waukan. A few of the neighbours met

every evening and performed the kind office of watchers. One of them at least had to be awake, lest the evil spirits might come and put a mark on the body. The time was ordinarily spent in reading the Scriptures, sometimes by one and sometimes by another of the watchers. Some of the passages usually read were the ninety-first Psalm, the fifteenth chapter of St. John's Gospel, and the fifteenth chapter of 1.Corinthians. Other passages were read besides these. All conversation was carried on in a suppressed voice.

The Rev James Napier found similar practices near Glasgow in 1879. He recalled: 'After death there came a new class of superstitious fears and practices. The clock was stopped, the looking-glass was covered with a cloth, and all domestic animals were removed from the house until after the funeral. These things were done, however, by many from the old custom, and without their knowing the reason why such things were done. Originally the reason for the exclusion of dogs and cats arose from the belief that, if either of these animals should chance to leap over the corpse, and be afterwards permitted to live, the devil would gain power over the dead person'.

Towards the end of the seventeenth century the practice known as 'chesting' became common practice. Its origin was in the Acts of Parliament aimed at encouraging trade in Scotland. In 1694 an Act designed to foster the linen industry ordained that the corpse should be shrouded in a sheet of plain linen without lace or point. In 1705 this Act was repealed and another passed ordering that every body should be swathed in plain Scots wollen cloth. In order to secure compliance with these laws Parliament instructed the nearest elder or deacon, with a neighbour or two 'should be present at the putting in of the dead corpse in the coffin, that they may see the same done'. From this rule arose the custom of 'kisting' when the devotional exercises were held by minister or elders as the body was transferred to the coffin.

Although funeral sermons were prohibted in 1638, the internment was a very public affair as noted by English naturalist, John Ray when he visited Scotland in the 1660s. 'When anyone dies, the sexton or bell-man goeth about the streets, with a small bell in his hand, which he tinkleth all along as he goeth, and now and then he makes a stand and proclaims who is dead, and invites the people to come to the funeral at such an hour. The people and minister many times accompany the corpse to the grave at the time appointed, with the bell before them, where there is nothing said, but only the corpse laid in.' Writing more than half a century later, the Reverend Dr Thomas Somerville of Jedburgh, recalled similar practices:

> ...in all the towns I was acquainted with, every death was immediately made known to the inhabitants by the passing bell. This was usually done by the beadle or kirk officer, who walked through the streets at a slow pace, tinkling a small bell, sometimes called the dead-bell, and sometimes the passing-bell, and, with head uncovered, intimated that a brother (or sister) whose name was given had departed this life... As the intimation made by the passing bell was understood to be a general invitation, great crowds attended the funeral. I may add, that at the time to which I refer, several of the female relatives walked in the rear of the funeral procession to the gate or threshold of the churchyard, where they always stopped and dispersed.

Register House. From James Grant, Old & New Edinburgh, *issued in weekly instalments c.1890.*

Women in the eighteenth century regarded a funeral as an occasion to wear their best clothes; they usually walked to the kirkyard gate at the rear of the funeral procession, to the gate or threshold of the churchyard leaving the men to follow to the grave. If a husband had lost a wife, the custom was for him to remain at home, presuming he was too overcome with grief to be able to follow the procession. In 1789, James Boswell, upon the death of his wife, writes 'It is not customary in Scotland for a husband to attend the funeral of his wife, but I resolved if I possibly could, to do the last honours myself.'

Although the Kirk disapproved of the superstition surrounding baptisms, marriages and funerals, the people had a strong attachment to tradition that went beyond the laws of the kirk or the state. This is demonstrated in an account taken from the *Scots Magazine* of 1785. The body of an old lady who had collapsed in front of her neighbours was treated with due respect and ceremony and funeral practices followed faithfully, perhaps too faithfully on this occasion. According to the account, 'Two of her neighbours who observed her fall, ran to her assistance, but her pulse was totally stopped. On Monday she was put in her coffin, and just as the joiner was about to do the last office the corpse changed colour, and had all the appearance of returning to life; notwithstanding which, they carried her to the grave and buried her.'

Chapter Two

LIFE IN THE COUNTRYSIDE

The Scottish countryside at the beginning of the eighteenth century appeared to those who visited it from south of the border a desolate and poverty-ridden place. An English tourist who travelled north of the border in 1702 found that the 'surface was generally unenclosed; oats and barley the chief grain products; wheat little cultivated; little hay made for winter, the horses then feeding chiefly on straw and oats.' The agricultural techniques of Scotland had hardly changed in centuries and the majority of those who lived in the countryside lived a hand to mouth existence that could be ended by bad weather and famine. By the end of the eighteenth century, however, a revolution would take place that would change the Scottish countryside for ever as the Lowlands were enclosed and the Highland's given over to sheep and cattle forcing many to emigrate or seek work in the flourishing towns.

The Scottish countryside until the eighteenth century was haunted by the spector of blight and famine. A bad harvest could mean misery and hunger for the poorer classes that swiftly led to famine conditions owing to the lack of transport and the difficulty of helping those living in remote parts. A parish priest recorded one such famine in 1571:

> On Feb. 22nd there came a great storm and snow and hail and wind, that nae man or beast might take up their heads, nor gang nor ride, and many beasts, and many men and women were perished in sundry parts, and all kind of vituals right dear, and that because nae mills might grind for the frost.

Of all the famines which devasted the Scottish countryside over the centuries that of the 1690s is the best documented. Seven years of bad

Pier at Ardrossan, Ayreshire. From William Daniell, Voyage Round Great Britain, *1820.*

weather and failed crops resulted in a famine so severe that a fifth of the Scots population – about 200,000 people – were reduced to begging. In some country areas it was said that a third or even half of the population died or emigrated. In 1699 Robert Sibbald described the suffering he saw all around him:

> For want some die in the wayside, some drop down in the streets, the poor sucking babs are starving for want of milk, which the empty breasts of their mothers cannot furnish them. Everyone may see Death in the face of the poor that abound everywhere; the thinness of their visage, their ghostly looks, their feebleness, their agues and their fluxes threaten them with sudden death if care be not taken of them. And it is not only common wandering beggars that are in this case, but many householders who lived well by their labour and their industry are now by want forced to abandon their dwellings.

As a result of this famine great tracts of the country formerly under cultivation were abandoned and would not be reclaimed for much of the following century. Many quitted the land to work or beg in towns and villages across Scotland, while many thousands fled to Ulster.

Life in the countryside, even in the better years, was hard and stern and the scarcity of money was everywhere apparent to the traveller. The signs of general poverty were to be seen in the houses of both high and low. The noble might live in a castle, the laird in a baronial tower or in one of the two-storeyed mansions that came in late in the seventeenth century, but it was an uncommonly prosperous farmer who could afford anything better than the traditional two-roomed cottage. Even the laird had uncarpeted wooden floors in most rooms, and the farmer bare earth or trampled rush or heather: all suffered from cold, damp and draughts, or suffocated from peat-smoke.

It was a very stratified society. At the top were the substantial landowners consisting of the nobles: dukes, marquises, earls, viscounts and barons. After them came the knights and baronets and then the lairds, whose hereditary titles were tied to the land. All such people were described as 'of' somewhere. The landowning class included most clan chiefs, some of whom were granted titles. Most landowners took no direct role in the cultivation of the land. The exception was 'bonnet lairds' who possessed small estates of a few hundred acres or less and were generally found in a band of country stretching from Fife in the east to Argyll in the west, but by the end of the eighteenth century their numbers were in serious decline. Edward Burt while visiting the Highlands in the early eighteenth century was amazed to find that even those with small landholdings took to naming themselves after their land: 'a single enclosed field, nearly adjoining to the suburbs of this town, containing, so near as I can guess, about five or six acres, called Fairfield. This to the owner gives the tile laird of Fairfield, and it would be a neglect or kind of affront to call him by his proper name, but only Fairfield. For those they call lairds in Scotland do not go by their surname; but, as in France, by the name of their house, estate, or part of it. But if the lordship be sold, the title goes along with it to the purchaser, and nothing can continue the name of it to the first possessor but mere courtesy'.

Only a minority of the rural population held a lease with many of these holding only a few acres of land. A tenant, often discribed in the records as 'possessor' or 'occupier' was not the owner of the land he worked. The lease (in Scots 'tack') commonly varied from nine to nineteen years with longer periods only beccomming more common by the second half of the eighteenth

The Coolin, taken from Loch Slapin. From William Daniell, Voyage Round Great Britain, *1820.*

century. The rental of the land was paid largely in kind, partly because money was extremely scarce in Scotland amongst every class. The rest of the rent was paid in so many bolls of meal, so many sheep, hens, eggs, butter and cheese, besides so many days' ploughing and reaping. The result of this method of payment was that landlords, though requently short of cash, required huge granaries to store their rents in kind. This may partially explain the legendary hospitality amongst the landed gentry who were burdened with superabundant supplies of grain, mutton, poultry and fish.

The majority of the rural population consisted of cottar families, sometimes referred in the records as 'pendiclers' or 'grassmen', who held a few acres from tenants in return for providing labour services for a number of days in the year and, occasionally, also making some rent payments. The homes of the cottars and crofters were humble as described by Thomas Kirke in 1679:

> The houses of the commonalty are very mean, mud-wall and to hatch the best; but the poorer sort lives in such miserable hutts as

never eye beheld; men, women and children pig together in a poor mouse-hold of mud, heath and some such like matter; in some parts where turf is plentiful they build up little cabins thereof with arched roofs of turf without a stick of timber in it; when their houses are dry enough to burn it serves them for fuel and they remove to another.

By the middle of the eighteenth century, the cottar class were increasingly condemned as idle and resistant to change and only the more ambitious tenants were rewarded with new leases. As one contemporary put it, 'It would be endless to state what is so often repeated in the surveys, that the small farm is found to be attended with an insufficient capital, with puny enclosures down to two acres and with wretched husbandry; that the poor farmer is always a bad one, the lower the rent the poorer the tenant, and with husbandry worse; that idleness and laziness prevail; that the small farm is not worth the attention of any man of ingenuity and property'.

At the bottom of the social standing in the countryside was the landless servant class consisting of both men and women. Single servants, the majority of the landless workers before 1750, were mainly young men and women in their late teens, and early twenties who lived with the farmer's family and were employed on contracts for periods of six months at a time. Many of them were born into cottar households before entering full-time service and at marriage some returned to the land by obtaining a cottar holding. According to a contemporary source in 1849:

Female servants form probably one twelve part of our whole population, this having a large influence, either for good or evil, according to their general character. They are generally strong and healthy; this may be attributed to their youth rather than to proper attentions to food, clothing etc. In other occupations are found persons of every age, but in this class few continue working as servants after they are 40 years of age, by the time they have reached that period of life they are married, or get into less laborious situations.

Many of them were hired at very low wages to pull turnips during the winter which provoked pity in many contemporary accounts. According to the same account:

Conceive a female having to work in the open air all day amidst perhaps drifting snow, drizzling sleet, or drenching rain, and this day after day. Is this fit and proper work for a woman? Add to this, those thus engaged are of the poorest class and not able to procure for themselves anything like comfortable clothing. Such a mode of life is sufficient to undermine the strongest female constitution and I have no doubt many are thereby ruined in health for life...

Women formed an important part of the labour force on the nineteenth-century farm. Their work kept the farmhouse and diary running smoothly. They were needed in the fields for tasks like weeding, thinning and gathering up harvested crops. Both spinning and weaving of wool and lint were also carried on by women in their own homes. In a letter of date 1680, and attributed to the Countess of Erroll of that time, it is said 'the women of this country are mostly employed spinning and working of stockings and making of plaiden webs, which the Aberdeen merchants carry over the sea;

A Domestic Scene. From Henry Grey Graham, The Social Life of Scotland in the Eighteenth Century. Adam & Charles Black, 1901

and it is this which bringeth money to the commons; other ways of getting it they have not.' A century later, the minister of Glenmuiek recorded in the *Old Statistical Acount*, with some emphasis, 'while I accuse the men of indolence, I should do great injustice to the women if I did [not] exempt them from the charge, by whose industry and diligence their families are in a great measure supported.'

Before the late eighteenth century, crops were grown in the runrig system: elongated s-shaped plots that were divided between the local community around the farm settlement in an intensively cultivated area known as the *infield*. Beyond this area was the less-intensively cultivated *outfield*, where livestock could be grazed on pastures. They were effectively islands of cultivation, surrounded by more infertile areas that were never tilled. With the land generally unlimed, unmanured and undrained it was often the case that the yield could not feed the inhabitants of the district, and tenants renting from forty to a hundred acres needed to buy meal for their families.

English visitors until well into the eighteenth century were struck by the open, unenclosed, hedgeless landscape that greeted them. There were few enclosures except round the gardens of gentlemen's houses; farms and fields were left entirely exposed over which cattle could wander at their will. Dr Johnson recalled in the 1770s:

> From the bank of the Tweed to St. Andrews I had never seen a single tree, which I did not believe to have grown up far within the present century. Now and then about a gentleman's house stands a small plantation, which in Scotch is called a policy, but of these there are few, and those few all very young. The variety of sun and shade is here utterly unknown. There is no tree for either shelter or timber. The oak and the thorn is equally a stranger, and the whole country is extended in uniform nakedness, except that in the road between Kirkaldy and Cowpar, I passed for a few yards between two hedges.

By the middle of the eighteenth century more enterprising landlords began to combine small tenancies into one farm and let to more substantial tenants who came under agreement, with a lease of nineteen years. Under the new conditions the fields were enclosed, ground was drained, limed and manured; waste ground was reclaimed from moor and marsh; hedges and dykes were raised; and miserable gray oats – or small corn – gave place to proflic grains; and potatoes and turnips in the field provided food for a rapidly expanding population.

The early attempts by more enterprising landlords to enclose the land encountered determined opposition from the poorer tenants who saw their right of pasturing cattle on common ground being infringed; many farmers were suspicious of their rents being raised and labourers were alarmed that their occupation as herds were being endangered. In the south, landlords who were determined to enclose their lands and stock them with black cattle, faced violent retaliation. So high was the general feeling that it evoked the following rhyme:

> *Against the poor the lairds prevail in all their wicked works,*
> *Who will enclose both hill and dale and turn cornfields to parks.*
> *The lords and lairds they drive us out*
> *From mailings where we dwell ;*
> *The poor man cries, where shall we go?*
> *The rich say go to hell.*

In Galloway tenants who were dispossed or under threat of eviction formed themselves into bands to destroy the enclosing walls and hedges during the summer of 1724. Order was restored and the ring leaders apprehended and taken to Kirkcudbright jail. They were tried at the Court of Justice in January 1725 and imprisoned. One of the enterprising landlords in the district, John Maxwell of Terraughty and Munches, who witnessed these events as a child later recalled: 'The spirit of insubordination shown by the Levellers having been put down, agricultural improvement advanced with rapid strides. The great work of enclosing was carried on with vigour, and the advantages of the system were generally felt and acknowledged'.

Most of those evicted from their holdings accepted their position stoically accepting work on the labour-entensive farms or in the growing industrial towns. Visiting Galloway during the 1720s, Daniel Defore commented: 'the common people all over this country, not only are poor, but look poor; they appear dejected and discourag'd, as if they had given over all hopes of ever being otherwise than what they are.' In contrast he found that the wealth of the area was in sheep, black cattle and horses. He found that 'the gentlemen generally take their rents in cattle, and some of them have so great a quantity, that they go to England with their droves, and take the money themselves. It is no uncommon thing for a Galloway nobleman to send 4000 sheep, and 4000 head of black cattle to England in a year, and sometimes more.'

The new breed of tenant who could pay the increased rents benefitted from the rising prices brought about by the demands of the rapidly expanding towns and cities which created a rapidly increasing market for provisions of all kinds. With this went an improvement in wages and in social condition. 'I travelled', wrote Roberston Agric of Perthshire in 1790, 'though some places where not many years ago the people were wretchedly poor, want sat upon every brow, hunger was painted on every face; neither their tattered clothes nor their miserable cottages were a sufficient shelter from the cold; now the labourers have put off the long clothing, the tardy pace, the lethargic look of their fathers, for the short doublet, the linen trousers, the quick pace of men who are labouring for their own behoof, and work up to the spirit of their cattle, and the rapid revolution of the threshing machine'.

Market Cross in a highland township. From Edward Burt, Letters from a Gentleman in the North of Scotland to his friend in London, *1754.*

The chief change in the countryman's diet and dress was noted by the compilers of the *New Statistical Account* (1834–45) was the appearance of tea, sugar and wheaten bread, usually as part of the afternoon meal, even in the humblest cottages. The minister of a Banffshire parish asserts that 'a very great change as to diet and dress has taken place during the forty years last past.' Prior to that era 'neither tea kettle nor tea could be found but in two families' in his parish. 'Two hats only appeared at church; a lady adorned herself with the plaid, and a gentleman was not ashamed of homespun clothing. But now most families drink tea once, many twice, a-day. The ploughman appears at church and market with his hat, linen, and good broad cloth, and it may be taken for granted that the country belles will exert themselves to outshine the country beaux.'

No such luxury was apparanent to visitors to the Scottish Highlands during the eighteenth and nineteenth century. Contemporary accounts of Scotland from the eighteenth century agree that the Highlands were over-populated with most of its inhabitants living on the edge of destitution. Thomas Pennant, who toured Skye in 1772, found that 'the poor are left to providence's care. They prowl like other animals along the shore to pick up limpets and other shellfish, the casual repasts of hundreds during part of the year in these unhappy islands'. John Leyden, in his *Tour of the Highlands and Western Isles* in 1800, wrote: 'The houses of the peasants in Mull are most deplorable. Some of the doors are hardly hour feet high and the houses themselves, composed of earthen sods, in many instances are scarcely twelve. There is often no other outlet of smoke but at the door, the consequence of which is that the women are more squalid and dirty than the men and their features more disagreeable'.

The land, once held by the clan in common, had by the eighteenth century becomes the chief's. Below the chief were the principal tenants, or tacksmen, who were his lieutenants in time of war. The tacksmen sublet the land they rented to sub-tenants. In return the sub-tenants provided service when required for a certain number of days each year to the tacksmen or chieftain, as well as for a rent generally paid in kind; by oatmeal, peat, eggs, or the like.

In general the Highland farming methods were similar to those that had prevailed in the Lowlands until the middle of the eighteenth century. The land in permanent use for agriculture consisted on the infield, nearest the farmstead, and the outfield, separated from the moorland by a head-dyke of stones or turf and itself usually divided into two portions. These consisted of the folds, generally the smaller area, in which the cattle were folded in the year before cropping to provide manure. They were then cropped until they yielded little return, when they were allowed to lie fallow for five or six years. There were also the faughs, generally the larger area, which never received any manure but were cropped in the same way.

As might be expected, the Highland tillers of the soil did not produce sufficient corn to enable them to sell any. On the contrary, the inhabitants of the glens and the islands were under the necessity of bringing in large quantities of meal, which, in the case of the southern Highlands, came from the Lowlands, and, in the case of the north and west, from the districts of the Moray, Beauly, and Cromarty Firths, and the county of Caithness. What they mainly relied on for a return in money was their live stock, consisting of cattle, horses, sheep, goats, and pigs, which found their way into the Lowlands and England. The herring and the potato were the staple foods of Highland life. It was a monotonous diet. The minister of Morvern, in south west Lochaber, recorded in the *New Statistical Account* in 1845: 'There are many, it is feared, much in the predicament of a little boy of the parish, who, on being asked on a certain occasion of what his three daily meals consisted gave the same unvarying answer, "mashed potatoes", and on being further asked by his too inquisitive enquirer, "what else?" replied with great artlessness but with evident surprise, "a spoon".

When the potato crop failed potential disaster faced the population. This happened on a local scale in Argyll in 1833, and recurred again over most of the west coast in 1836 and 1837, threatening mass starvation which was only staved off by prompt charitable action of the part of the relief committees organized in London, Glasgow and other towns. Far eclipsing any of these in seriousness, however, was the famine precipitated by the blight of 1846, which wiped out the potato crop of the entire west coast: some 150,000 people were at risk. Once again charity was remarkably quick off the mark in sending relief, and the London Government (in contrast to its inefficiency in Ireland) organized the distribution of food and seed corn from depot ships stationed in the principal firths. The chief government relief co-ordinator, the appropriately named Sir Edward Pine Coffin, cajoled and bullied local landowners to accept at least minimal responsibility towards their tenants, so that direct deaths from hunger were kept extremely low and even deaths through hunger-induced diseases such as typhus failed to show much of an increase.

There was therefore compelling economic reasons for introducing sheep to many hard-pressed estates in the Highlands. Few, however, believed that low-land sheep would survive a Highland winter. The Cheviot, a tough, black-faced breed which yielded consistently more wool and meat than its northern rivals, changed this view. In 1791, Sir John Sinclair introduced the first sheep in the far north on the Langwell estate in Caithness. Sir John argued that the native Highlanders should be absorbed into this new economy, but his advice was generally ignored. In the *Statistical Account of Scotland*, published in 1825, Sir John regretted the conversion of large tracts of the county into sheep-farms and was concerned 'to see a few shepherds strolling over the face of a country, which formerly was the nurse of heroes, the bulwarks of their native soil, every ready to brave danger and death in its defence'.

To make way for the sheep, Landlords evicted their tenants by the thousands. It seems amazing that the Highlanders so rarely resisted eviction by landlords. In Ireland there was often trouble in parts of the country where similar clearances took place, but the Scots generally submitted peacefully to their fate. It helped that their landlord was usually the clan chief and often a blood relation. Their ignorance of the English language also prevented people from making their grievances widely known. In addition, with few exceptions, Presbyterian ministers defended the landlords, from whom they received their Highland parishes, threatening the people with damnation if they did not obey the writs of eviction.

Some did resist. However, in 1792, the men of Ross and Sutherland banded together to try to stop the steady invasion of sheep over what they regarded as their ancestral lands. In July, 400 men of Ross started from Lairg and marched south driving the Lowland shepherds who had come north with their flocks and their sheep in front of them. They had nearly reached Alness when word arrived that three companies of the Black Watch were looking for them. They quickly dispersed into the surrounding countryside and when the soldiers arrived there was no sign of them. Five men were eventually tried and sent to Botany Bay. It was not until 1813 that there was another attempt at resistance. During the previous year, tenants at the Strath of Kildonan, part of the vast Sutherland estate, were given notice to quit their dwellings and the areas was divided into three sheep farms. In March 1813 Mr Reid, the Northumbrian manager of a southern sheep farm, visited the area, but later claimed he was attacked by a mob of angry people. A detachment of infantry was summoned from Fort George to calm the situation.

Two of the most notorious evictors were Patrick Sellar and James Loch. Sellar and Edinburgh-trained advocate, was factor of the Sutherland estates

Remains of the chapel etc on Inch. From William Daniell, Voyage Round Great Britain, *1820.*

and tenant of the Kildonan and Farr lands. He supervised the eviction of some 2,000 people in 1814 – long remembered in the Highlands as the 'Year of the Burning'. Accompanied by constables and sheriff officers, Sellar gave tenants half an hour to clear their furniture before setting the dwellings on fire. According to witnesses 'to this plan they ruthlessly adhered'. When he came to the house of William Chisholm, he found a bed-ridden woman nearly one hundred years old. Chisholm pleaded that his mother-in-law was too ill to be removed. Sellar is said to have replied "Damn her, the old witch; she has lived too long. Let her burn!" The house was set on fire and the blankets were in flames before she could be got out. She was placed in a little shed where she died five days later. The Sheriff-Substitute of Sutherland, Robert Kid, indicted Sellar on charges of murder and arson. The trial took place in English, which was incomprehensible to most of the Gaelic-speaking witnesses, and the jury, composed mostly of local landowners, found Sellar 'not guilty'.

Sellar retired from the Duke of Sutherland's services in 1819 but the evictions continued under the supervision of James Loch. Writing in 1820,

Loch justified the clearances as natural and logical. 'The coast of Sutherland abounds with many different kinds of fish, not only sufficient for the consumption of the country but affording a supply for more distant markets, when cured and salted. It seemed as if it had been pointed out by Nature that the system for this remote district was to convert the mountainous districts into sheep-walks, and to remove the inhabitants to the coast'. In 1819, Loch authorised the Strath-naver Clearances that saw the eviction of 2,000 Highlanders. One eyewitness, Donald MacLeod, reported that at 11 o'clock one night he climbed a hill and counted: '250 blazing houses. Many of the owners were my relatives and all of whom I personally knew; but whose present condition, whether in or out of the flames, I could not tell. The fires lasted six days, till the whole of the dwellings were reduced to ashes of smoking ruins. During one of those days a boat lost her way in the dense smoke as she approached the shore; but at night she was enabled to reach a landing place by the light of the flames'.

Twenty-five years after the clearances in Sutherlandshire, accounts of the eviction of the Rosses from Gleanvalvie finally reached the national press. In May 1845, *The Times* reported that eighteen families had been evicted by the factor James Gillanders on behalf of the absentee laird of Kindeace. Many were now ecamped in the graveyard of Croick Free Church. Behind the church families huddled under tarpaulin stretched over poles, the sides closed in with horse cloths, rugs, blankets and plaids. There were 23 children in the churchyard, all under the age of ten and seven of them were ill. Some of the people starched brief messages on the diamond-paned windows of the church: Glencalvie people was in the church here May 24, 1845: 'John Ross shepherd'; 'Glencalvie is a wilderness, ship blow them to the colony'. The church would alter became a place of pilgrimage for those who wished to trace their ancestors back to Ross county.

By the end of the Famine the old way of life in the Highlands had been virtually destroyed. In less than three generations the ancient Gaelic communities had been eliminated. Many had emigrated; others had followed their Lowland counterparts into the towns and cities in search or employment. The 500,000 persons engaged in agriculture, forestry and horticulture in 1821, forming about one in four of the population, had dwindled by 1861 to 350,000 or less than one in eight. Although the total population of Scotland more than doubled between 1821 and 1911 – rising from 2,091, 521 to 4, 760, 103 – those counties which depended mainly on agriculture were actually losing inhabitants.

For many of those who remained on the land faced a life of hardship and poverty enlivened only by the tourists who flocked from south of the border encouraged Sir Walter Scott's recreation of Scotland's past and Queen Victoria's love for all things Scottish. In the introduction to *The Wild Sports and Natural History of the Highlands* published in 1892 the author complained of this intrusion: 'The railways driven far into wastes of trackless bog and heather, now admit countless tourists to the most retired districts. Their taste for shooting and fishing, and the charm of a freer life than can be found in the great cities, have planted castles and shooting lodges all over Scotland.' No wonder the evicted stonemason Donald Macleod should be so scornful of the 100ft statue raised in honour of the Duke of Sutherland near Golspie in north-east Scotland. 'All who could raise a shilling gave it', he later wrote from his exile in Canada, 'and those who could not awaited in terror for the consequences of their default'.

Chapter Three

LIFE IN THE TOWNS AND CITIES

For much of its history, Scotland had little need for large settlements. Throughout most of the country its inhabitants led a pastoral life with small-scale settlements dependent on summer grazing of cattle away from permanent dwellings. This changed with the Norman settlement of Lowland Scotland from the twelfth century when Scottish kings established a series of royal burghs as military, administrative and commercial centres. Another wave of urban development took place during the second half of the eighteenth century when the Industrial Revolution created a demand for labour. By 1851, one in five Scots lived in the four cities of Glasgow, Edinburgh, Dundee and Aberdeen, and by 1911 the ratio had risen to one in three. With 50 per cent of the population living in towns of 20,000 or more, Scots were a more urbanized nation than any other in the world except for the English.

The emergence of major settlements in Scotland received a major boost in the mid-eleventh century, when David I encouraged a string of Norman newcomers to the new towns which he had founded or encouraged; Stirling, Roxburgh, Berwick and Edinburgh flourished attracting English and Continental merchants. These early Scottish towns, or Royal burghs, developed as centres for the marketing of any surplus produce, and as bases for the various craftsmen whose skills were relevant to the land including smiths, masons, farmers, weavers. These burghs also held a monopoly for foreign trade, import and export, which no lesser burgh could infringe; and Royal burghs sent commissioners to the Scottish parliament. Apart from Royal Burghs other burghs, like Greenock or Kilmarnock, developed the estates of the great landowners. If a burgh was on church land – like Dunfermline, Arbroath, St Andrews, Paisley or Glasgow – it was an ecclesiastical burgh, its charter coming from the Abbot.

Kings saw the granting of royal charters as useful political opportunities, and granted them in areas where they knew themselves to be popular. King James III therefore gave charters to many of the small towns around the Moray coast, and James IV raised improbably small Fife villages to Royal burgh status. Burghs evolved their own law to govern trading transactions, and disputes could be referred to the Court of the Four Burghs (originally Berwick, Edinburgh, Roxburgh, and Stirling). Many of the original townspeople, or burgesses, were newcomers to Scotland. At Berwick, the great trading town of the thirteenth century, Flemish merchants had their own Red Hall which they defended to the death against English attack in 1296.

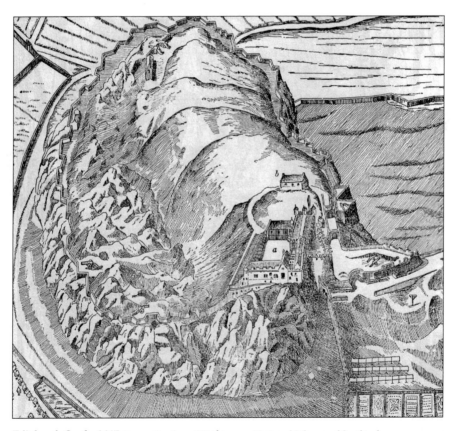

Edinburgh Castle, 1647. James Gordon of Rothiemay, National Library of Scotland.

The tron, or public weighing place, and the market cross formed the centre of the official life of the burgh. It was from here that official proclamations were made, a very necessary act during the centuries when most people were illiterate, and where Merchants conducted business. Life in a medieval Burgh, like that in the surrounding countryside, was very stratified with merchants living on the ground floor, the well-to-do on the first floor and descending upwards to the poorest in the attic. By the eighteenth century the rich began to move out to their own quarters, most notably in Edinburgh. William Creech commented in 1792 'people of quality and fashion lived in houses, which, in 1783, were inhabited by tradesmen, or by people in humble and ordinary life. The Lord Justice Clerk Tinwald's house was possessed by a French Teacher, Lord President Craigie's houses by a Rouping-wife or Sales-woman of old furniture, the house of the late President Dunda is now possessed by an iron-monger'.

The four major Scottish cities of the early nineteenth century, Edinburgh, Glasgow, Aberdeen and Dundee, were all ancient and important burghs. Early Edinburgh was a small settlement on the eastern side of the fortified rock overshadowed by the thriving port of Berwick and the royal retreats of Perth and Sterling. The loss of Berwick to the English in 1482, allowed Edinburgh to become the principal port between the Border and the Tay. Trade was carried out largely across the North Sea with the Low Countries and the Baltic through Leith, the port two miles from the town. Merchants using Leith had to reside in Edinburgh and the charter granted by Robert I to the city in 1329 included the port.

Edinburgh dominated Scotland's trade in wool and hides from the Lothians and the Mersey. It also exported more than half the coal sent from Scotland. At this time many of the city's burgesses were descendants of French, Flemish and English craftsmen planted there during the reign of David I. From the reign of James VI (1567–1625) onwards, the court came to spend most of its time at the Palace of Holyroodhouse. Begun in the 1430s it was remoddled for Mary, Queen of Scots, and her consort Henry, Lord Darnley who entwined initials can be seen above one of the doorways. Feuding nobles and lairds became a feature of court life and gun battles in the streets were not uncommon.

Aberdeen grew up as two separate burghs, Old Aberdeen – the cathedral and university town at the mouth of the Don – and 'New' Aberdeen (confusingly as ancient as 'Old' Aberdeen) the fishing and trading settlement where the creek of the Denburn entered the estuary of the Dee.

Until the arrival of the railway in 1850, Aberdeen provided virtually the only outlet for the surplus produce of the surrounding counties. Its relative isolation was an important factor in the development of the town serving the needs of the region and undertaking extensive trade with the Baltic, Poland and the Netherlands. When the Bishop of Meath, Richard Pococke, toured Scotland in the middle of the eighteenth century he found that Aberdeen had 'a great Export of Kit Stockings, Oat Meal, barley, Salmon , and some pickled pork, but not so much as formerly'. There was hardly a seaport in Germany or the Low Countries or Scandinavia where communities of Aberdonian merchants could not be found. As a result there is to be found in the local dialect not only native Pictish and Gaelic words and names, but also words brought in by trade with Danes, Norwegians, Swedes, Germans, Dutch and French.

Glasgow cathedral now stands on the site of St Kentigern's humble foundation to the northeast of the city on the side of the valley of the Molindinar Byrn. Bishop Jocelin, sometime between 1175 and 1178 obtained the royal charter which authorised the creation of a burgh at Glasgow and during the thirteenth and fourteenth centuries the political influence of Glasgow's bishops secured further royal grants and privileges. Nevertheless, for much of its early history, Glasgow remained a cathedral town on the wrong side of Scotland for Continental trade and could scarcely compete even with the minor commercial centres dotted along the east coast.

Dundee also has a long and remarkable history. A mile or so north of the town is Dundee Law, the plug of an extinct volcano and, at 571 ft, the city's highest point. An Iron Age fort, Dun Diagh or Diagh's Fort, from which the town may have derived its name, once occupied the site. Evidence exists of a settlement during the Roman period and later in AD 834 Kenneth MacAlpine used the Dundee area as a base from which he set out to conquer the Picts and make himself the first King of the Scots. The first reference to a more substantial settlement is recorded in 1054 and by the twelfth century Dundee was a well established town. King William I 'the Lion' granted Dundee a royal charter in the late twelfth century because his brother David, Earl of Huntingdon, had lands in the neighbourhood. By the fourteenth century Dundee was a prosperous port trading wool, sheepskins and cattlehides with the continental market. Trade was established with Flanders and the Baltic and all goods bought in Flanders had first to be exposed for sale in Dundee.

In the Highlands, towns were the exception rather than the rule. By the end of the nineteenth century Inverness remained the largest burgh, far ahead of other urban growths such as Dingwall, Oban, Stornoway, Fort William and Thurso, where the population did not exceed a few thousand. Inverness, a the long-established centre of the Highlands, was the capital of the Pictish kingdom of King Brude, who was visited and converted by St Columba c. 565. By the twelfth century Inverness had become a burgh nestling under the castle attributed to King Malcolm III Canmore, which remained a royal residence and fortress for centuries. When visiting Inverness, Captian Edward Burt noted in the eighteenth century:

> ... the natives do not call themselves Highlanders, not so much on account of their low situation, as because they speak English'. However he pointed out that 'although they speak English, there are scarce any who do not understand the Irish tongue; and it is necessary that they should do so, to carry on their dealings with the neighbouring country people; for within less than a mile of the town, there are few who speak any English at all.

Many Scottish towns and cities were greatly affected by the religious upheavals of the seventeenth century. Both Aberdeen and Dundee were sacked by an army commanded by the Marquis of Montrose. In 1655 Parliament sent commissioners to Scotland to report on the state of the country. One such was Thomas Tucker, Register to the Commissioners for the Excise in England who was sent to give his assistance in settling the excise and customs north of the border. 'The towne of Dundee', he recorded 'was sometime a towne of riches and trade, but the many rencontres it hath mett with all in the time of domestick comotions, and her obstinacy and pride of late yeares rendring her a prey to the soldier, have much shaken and abated her former grandeur; and notwithstanding all, shee remaynes still, though not glorious, yett not contemptible.'

The towns and cities had recovered by the early eighteenth century and the next two centuries were marked by economic expansion. Daniel Defoe visited Aberdeen during the early 1720s and found its market-place 'very beautiful and spacious' and the adjacent streets 'very handsome and well built, the houses lofty and high; but not so as to be inconvenient, as in Edinburgh; or low, to be contemptible, as in most other places. But the generality of the citizens' houses are built of stone four story high, handsome

The tollbooth. From James Grant, Old & New Edinburgh, *issued in weekly instalments c.1890.*

sash-windows, and are very well furnish'd within, the citizens here being as gay, as genteel, and, perhaps, as rich, as in any city in Scotland'.

From the middle of the seventeenth century Edinburgh became the professional and intellectual capital of Scotland. By 1694, professionals outnumbered merchants with more than 200 legal professionals alone. Most of its inhabitants, rich and poor lived in the Old Town which sprawls down the hill from the Castle to the Palace of Holyroodhouse and the adjacent abbey, a stretch known as the Royal Mile. 'The old town', wrote Dorothy Wordsworth, sister of the poet, 'with its irregular houses, stage above stage, seen as we saw it, in the obscurity of a rainy day, hardly resembles the work of man, it is more like a piling up of rocks'. Thomas Morer, who visited the Old Town in 1689 was struck by the fact that the stone houses were 'so lofty, that five or six stories is an ordinary height, and one row of buildings there is near the Parliament Close with no less than fourteen. The reason of it is, their scantness of room, which, not allowing 'em large foundations, they are forced to make it up in the superstructure, to entertain comers, who are very desirous to be in, or as near as they can to the city'.

The Old Town was overcrowded with no sewers, simply ditches at the sides of the street to carry away the waste. Those who lived in the upper storeys of the tenements would throw their slops out of the window with a cry of 'Gardyloo!' (from the French Garde de l'eau! Meaning 'Beware of the water!') The novelist Daniel Defoe wrote: 'In a Morning, earlier than seven o'Clock, before the human Excrements are swept away from the doors, it stinks intolerably; for, after Ten at Night, you run a great Risque, if you walk the streets, of having Chamber-pots of Ordure thrown upon your Head'. Little wonder that the city earned the nickname of *Auld Reekie*.

Between 1770 and 1800 the population of Edinburgh doubled to 80,000 and continued its dramatic rise until the end of the nineteenth century. By the latter half of the eighteenth century, Edinburgh, growing in population and prosperity, began to find the constriction of life in the Old Town on the Rock intolerable. But large obstacles lay in the way of expanding north – the 'Nor' Loch', a considerable sheet of water immediately below the Castle and the Old Town, where Princes Street Gardens lie today. The Town Council drained the loch and three the North Bridge over the marshy land to the east of it. They then started to build the New Town to the design of James Craig. Craig had originally planned that terraced houses would be laid out in the form of a Union Jack but this was wisely modified into a grid of streets, focused upon two squares.

Those who could afford it left the Old Town for the space and cleanliness of the New Town. The Two Edinburghs existed side by side. More and more people were crammed into the old houses, some of which were now over three centuries old, to live in hunger and disease. Robert Louis Stevenson had a clear view of the social divisions of the city and in *Edinburgh: Picturesque Notes*, published in 1878 he wrote: 'there is not so much a blade of grass between the rich and the poor. To look over the South Bridge and see the Cowgate below full of crying hawkers, is to view one rank of society from another in the twinkling of an eye'.

The era of Georgian town planning was opened in Glasgow by the tobacco barons who built their elegant residences around George Square between 1750 and 1775. Other streets followed, topically named Virginia, Havannah and Jamaica Streets. The Aberdeen New Streets Act of 1800 had ushered in a half century of construction in Aberdeen. The most dramatic change was the creation of the mile-long Union Street in 1801 (named after the union of the British and Irish Parliament that year). Its creation was a massive engineering operation which at first, threatened to bankrupt the

Tavern Scene. From John Kay, A Series of Original Portraits, With Biographical Sketches and Illustrative Anecdotes. Edinburgh: A C Black, 1877

city. From 1817 to 1827 the burgh could not meet the interest charges on the huge loans raised to finance the work and the city was only rescued by the boom in trade.

Meanwhile outside the burghs there were relatively few populous towns. Most Scots lived in small fermtouns and survived on the produce grown in the immediate neighbourhood. The fermtoun was a cluster of farm houses, outbuildings and cot-houses, usually grouped without a formal plan. Eward Burt commented as he travelled north from Glasgow: 'One thing I observed of almost all the towns that I saw in a distance, which was, that they seemed large, and made a handsome appearance: but when I passed through them, there appeared a meanness which discovered the condition of the inhabitants: and all the out-skirts, which served to increase the extent of them at a distance, were nothing but the ruin of little houses, and these in pretty great number'. When he was asked whey he was told that 'when one of those houses was grown old and decayed, they often did not repair it, but, taking out the timber, they let the walls stand as a fit enclosure for a cale-yard (i.e. a little garden for coleworts), and that they built anew upon another street'.

In all towns the wooden galleries fronting the houses and many thatched roods made fire an ever-present menace. Dunfermline was devastated in 1624, Glasgow in 1652 and again in 1677, Kelso in 1684. Local regulations imposed severe penalties upon careless conduct and dangerous trades, such as the use of baking-ovens or the making of candles, in densely peopled tenements. Parliament in 1681 ordered the removal of all thatched roofs in Edinburgh, Glasgow, Aberdeen, Dundee and Stirling, and their replacement by slate or tile; but thatch, as the readiest and cheapest of roofing materials, lingered on into the nineteenth century even in the largest towns.

If fire was the chief threat to the life of the community, the greatest risk to its health and well-being lay in the almost universal indifference to sanitation and ordinary cleanliness. The town-dweller was often a crofter, with a kailyard or a back-garden, and perhaps a small, arable holding, and he valued, as fertiliser, the dung-heap piled up on the street before his house. As late as 1725 the fuilyie (street-garbage) of Leith was 'rouped' (or let by auction) for five years for the sum of £121 10s., the 'tacksman' or lessee undertaking in return for this fertiliser, to keep the streets clean.

Slaughterhouses and fish markets were a particular nuisance in towns, for butchers sometimes slaughtered in booths attached to their dwelling houses. At the same time the blood, bone and soap boiler, the tallow and fat melter, the tanner and lue manufacturer all plied their trade to the general discomfort of their fellow townsfolk. This can be seen in a vivid description of Glasgow Green at the end of the eighteenth century:

> The dung of the Slaughter-House and the intestines of slaughtered animals were collected in heaps, and allowed to remain for months together, till putrefaction took place, to the great annoyance of the neighbourhood. A gluework, and a work in which tharm was manufactured from the intestines of animals ina recent state, was erected at the bottom of the Laigh Green; and to complete the nuisance, the adjoining houses were occupied for cleaning tripe; and rees were fitted up for the retail of coal and coal-culm. The space on the bank of the river at the cattle market, came now to be used by the police as a receptacle for filfth from the streets.

Although efforts were made to keep the towns clean, little could be done until sewage and draingage systems could be improved. The Cowgate in Edinburgh had only surface drains till the 1840s when a committee of private gentlemen built an underground sewer to the Foul Buyrn. The drains in the closes were still very poor in the 1860s because the tenements were so subdivided and in such poor condition that it was difficult to join them up to the common sewer. The Royal Commission on the Sewage of Towns heard in evidence that the river the Water of Leith received the sewage of 100,000 people, 'the bed of the Water of Leith is rocky and uneven, and in the pools thus formed much of the solid matter conveyed by the sewage stagnates, and, passing into a state of puterescence, evolves abundantly offensive gases'. Most other towns were little different. Glasgow's first sewer was built in 1790. The nineteenth-century streets in Aberdeen had large common sewers though there were still many cesspools.

A supply of clean water was also essential to the health of the town. Water was generally collected from a well or standpipe in the street, the supply being restricted to a few hours two or three times a week, or it was bought from hawkers in the street. In Dumfries, the supply of good water was often problematic:

> With the exception of what was furnished by a few wells and private pumps, all the water used for domestic purposes was carried by hand or carted in barrels from the Nith by four old men, who doled it out in tin pitchers or cans, from door to door, at the rate of five capfuls a penny. The river, when swelled by heavy rains, which was often the case, became thick with mud; and it was constantly exposed to a more noxious pollution, caused by the refuse poured into it from the town. The quality of the water did not improve by being borne about in barrels of suspicious aspect; and often, indeed, the liquid drawn from them during summer acquired a taste-me-not repulsiveness by the presence of innumerable little objects, pleasant to no one save an enthusiast in entomology.

In the major cities like Edinburgh or Glasgow the situation was considerably worse. James Simpson, giving evidence in January 1847, when asked about the poorer classes in Edinburgh replied: 'Living, many of them, in floors of very high altitudes, they labour, particularly when sickness is in their families, under privation so great that they content themselves with a driblet of water that would surprise you – probably their little tea-kettle full.

Greenock, on the Clyde. From William Daniell, Voyage Round Great Britain, *1820.*

Anything like personal cleanliness in such a condition is rare, while domestic cleanliness is quite out of the question. Their recourse to public wells is not only a very great hardship on themselves, but is a source of public nuisance, moral as well as physical. I should be sorry to see any attempt to increase the number of these wells; and I hope to live to see the time when they will be a matter of history alone'.

By the eighteenth century many improving landlords began to develop towns and villages on their estates and they were determined to create model communities free from many of the problems associated with the older towns and cities. In the eighteenth century more than a hundred were established, either by enlarging the existing nucleus of homes or by building on a 'green field' site. They arranged geographically from Lybster and Sarclet in Caithness, which were established as fishing stations late in the century, to Cromarty which was planned as a renovated town in 1772. Most were on the eastern side of the country, but there were some twenty or so in the area around Glasgow and a dozen in the southwest between Port William and Newcastleton on the border. A few new villages were also created on the west coast, at Ullapool and Tobermory. The process went on into the next century with one of the last to be established being Edzell in 1839.

Some landowners, motivated by the need to create centres of consumption for local produce, established new communities. This was the case in the founding of Cuminestown in Buchan in 1763. According to the *Old Statistical Account* for Monquhitter parish, Aberdeenshire:

> Joseph Cumine of Auchry ... observing his tenants were frequently at a loss for a market, he determined to establish a permanent one on his own estates. For this purpose, he planned a regular village ... upon the Moorish part of a farm which in whole yielded only £11 a year. For a while, he felt in silence the sneers of his neighbours, who reprobated his scheme as wild and impracticable, but these temporary sneers soon gave way to lasting esteem. He prevailed on a few to take feus; he assisted the industrious with money; obtaining premiums for the manufacturer ... Settlers annually flocked to Cuminestown and the village, built of free-stone, soon assumed a flourishing appearance. In connection with some neighbouring gentlemen, he established in his village a linen manufacturer.

As the cotton industry prospered in Renfrewshire a series of planned industrial towns were built to serve its needs. Though some places, like New Lanark, remained no more than company villages others mushroomed into towns. In 1780 a co-partnership of Glasgow and Lancashire merchants built a cotton mill on the River Levern in Neilston parish, and at the same time 2km to the south, Gavin Rawlston feued off the new town of Newton Rawlston which became Barrhead. According to the *Glasgow Free Press*, for 8 September 1827:

> Barrhead, you must understand, has undergone a considerable metamorphosis with these thirty years back, when it may be said it was in its infancy; then it consisted of thirty families, now there is a street half a mile in length, built on each side ... there was perhaps but one small cotton factory on the Levern, and now there are six large ones within 2½ miles of each other, besides three or four printfields, two weaving factories, and bleachfields numerous and extensive. Thirty years ago there was only one public house in this village and now there are certainly thirty. Thirty years ago there was but one school in it, and now there are in the village and neighbourhood six or seven.

The Industrial Revolution in Scotland also revitalised some old established towns and villages. At Blairgowrie, for example, the abundant supply of water power led to the establishment of eleven mills employing 463 people. Some employees lived beside the mill in tied houses but more lived in the town itself. According to the *Imperial Gazetteer of Scotland*:

> A little after the beginning of the present century, Blairgowrie was an insignificant village of mean thatched houses; but now it has a decided town appearance, with good streets, many good houses, and a considerable stir of business ... A good deal of business is done in the town, and much employment given to the inhabitants in connection with the spinning-mills.

While textiles provided the economic base to the first industrial towns, iron and steel gave rise to fewer but more substantial towns. The lighting of the first coal burning furnace at Carron in 1760 heralded a revolution in iron-making. Carron was soon the largest foundry in Europe. A new settlement sprang up at Stenhousemuir, and Larbert changed from a small agricultural hamlet to an industrial town. Motherwell is another example of a new town which sprang up around several industries. According to F H Gromme, in his *Ordnance Gazetteer of Scotland* published in 1903 Motherwell was:

> Founded in the early years of the nineteenth century, having previously had no existence even as a village, it consists largely of the dwellings of miners and operatives employed in the neighbouring collieries and ironworks, and serves, in connection with the railway junctions, as a great bustling centre of traffic ... No Scottish town has grown so rapidly as Motherwell, such growth being due tom the vast extension of its mineral industries.

The industrial staple towns and some of the cities were most likely to suffer the adverse consequences of expansion which are often associated with urbanisation at this time. Such places as Paisley, Kilmarnock, Falkirk and Hawick grew swiftly, and their mainly working-class inhabitants were usually heavily concentrated in one or two industries which were often geared to overseas markets and hence were vulnerable to the changes in demand for international commodities. As part of the Chadwick Report of

Aberdeen Union Street. From a postcard. Author's collection

1842 examining the living conditions of the poor, Dr W L Lawrie, a doctor in Greenock, described this notoriously filthy town:

> The great proportion of the dwellings of the poor are situated in very narrow and confined closes or alleys leading from the main streets; these closes end generally in a cul-de-sac, and have little ventilation, the space between the houses being so narrow as to exclude the action of the sun on the ground. I might almost say there are no drains in any of these closes, for where I have noticed sewers, they are in such a filthy and obstructed state, that they create more nuisance than if they never existed. In those closes where there is no dunghill, the exrementitious and other offensive matter in thrown into the gutter before the door, or carried out and put in the street …

As he passed through one of the poorest districts of the town 'a little girl ran after me and requested me to come and see her mother as she could not keep her in bed; I found the mother lying in a miserable straw bed with a piece of carpet for a covering, delirious from fever; the husband, who was a drunkard, had died in the hospital of the same disease. There was no fire in the grate; some of the children were out begging, and the two youngest were crawling on the wet floor; it was actually a puddle in the centre, as the sewer before the house was obstructed, and the moisture made its way to the middle of the floor by passing under the door. Every saleable piece of furniture had been pawned during the father's illness for the support of the family. None of the neighbours would enter the house; the children were actually starving, and the mother was dying without any attendance whatever.'

The major cities also developed rapidly and encountered similar extremes of wealth and poverty. By the beginning of the nineteenth century Glasgow had one of the fastest growing populations in the United Kingdom. The massively unequal distribution of wealth meant that the splendid mansions in the West End were a marked contrast to the wynds and closes of the High Street, Saltmarket and Gallowgate areas in the East End where an estimated 20,000 people were crammed into dilapidated housing where sanitation was virtually non-existent. In 1886 in Glasgow, a third of families lived in one room:

> In some rooms may be found a superfluity of articles – old beds, tables, chairs, boxes, pots, and dishes, with little regard to order or cleanliness. In others, a shakedown in the corner, a box or barrel for a table, a broken stool, an old pot or pan, with a few dishes. In many rooms, no furniture at all; and the whole family, including men, women and children, huddled together at night on such straw or rags as they can gather.

Dr J B Russell, the Medical Officer of Health for Glasgow, said of the children whose deaths were so numerous in this vile environment: 'Their little bodies are laid on a table or on a dresser so as to be somewhat out of the way of their brothers and sisters, who play and sleep and eat in their ghastly company. From the beginning to rapid-ending the lives of these children are short. One in every five of all who are born there never see the end of their first year.' For many in the industrial towns and cities only a few generations earlier their ancestors had left the highly stratified society of the countryside for the promise of higher wages and greater freedom. They found themselves instead once again at the bottom of the social order in the sort of poverty that their descendants would find difficult to image.

Chapter Four

CLANS AND KINSHIP

Scotland at the beginning of the eighteenth century remained a country divided by tradition, language and culture. In the eighteenth century, Edward Burt noted the Lowland attitudes to their northern neighbours: 'The Highlanders are but little known even to the inhabitants of the low country of Scotland, for they have ever dreaded the difficulties and dangers of travelling among the mountains; and when some extraordinary reason has obliged any one of them to such a progress, he has, generally speaking, made his testament before he set out, as though he was entering upon a long and dangerous sea voyage, wherein it was very doubtful if he should ever return.' Yet, for centuries the Border country had much in common with the Highlands, with its warring families. By the seventeenth century, both Highland and Lowland were subjugated by an increasingly powerful government and the old way of life was further undermined by landlords who replaced the warrior with sheep and black cattle.

In 1792, when he was still young lawyer waiting to enter the Bar, Sir Walter Scott made a walking tour of the Border country: Rosebank, Upper Tyneside, and the Cheviot and Eildon Hills. This countryside of rolling hills, forests and ruined abbeys had been a violent place that had known centuries of battles and 'reiving wars' between Lowlanders and the English, and among Lowland clans such as the Douglasses, the Maxwells and Homes. Scott heard and wrote down a number of the ancient 'riding ballads' giving these violent warrior clans a romantic place in Scottish history.

By the time of Scott's visit all that was left of the old border society were the stories and yet for more than four centuries it had been the toughest and most lawless quarter in Britain, once known as the Debateable Land. Since the War of Independence, when both Scottish and English armies had laid

Border Reiver. 'Auld Wat of Harden' by Tom Scott RSA.

the Borders waste time after time, the hardy and rugged people on both sides of the Border learned to live on the move. Bishop Leslie of Ross, gave an account of sixteenth century Reiver life, which was tinged with a degree of sympathy for the poverty of the people His description of sixteenth century border life is oddly reminiscent of accounts of the Scottish Highlands over the next two centuries. According to Bishop Leslie the border clans

> assume to themselves the greatest habits of license. For as, in time of war, they are readily reduced to extreme poverty by the almost daily inroads of the enemy, so, on the restoration of peace, they entirely neglect to cultivate their lands, though fertile, from the fear of the fruits of their labour being immediately destroyed by a new war. Whence it happens that they seek their subsistence by robberies or rather by plundering and rapine, for they are particularly adverse to the shedding of blood; nor do they much concern themselves whether it be from Scots or English that they rob and plunder.

Crops of oats, rye and barley were tilled in the spring and summer but mostly the people raised cattle and sheep. An English traveller who stayed in the home of a Border knight in 1598 observed that 'they commonly eat hearth cakes of oats and although he was entertained 'after their best manner' he found 'no art of cookery or household stuff, but rude neglect of both'. He goes on, 'Many servants brought in the meat, with blue caps on their heads, the table being more than half furnished with great platters of porridge, each having a little sodden meat. When the table was served, the servants sat down with us; but the upper mess instead of porridge, had a pullet with some prunes in the broth. The Scots, living then in factions, used to keep many followers and so consumed their revenues in victuals, and were always in want of money.'

The word 'reive' means to rob or plunder. The border peoples on both sides of the border took to raiding livestock, and, when possible, returned with money, goods, and even people who would be held to ransom. According to Bishop Leslie there was '...a persuasion that all property is common by law of nature, and is therefore liable to be appropriated by them in their necessity.' In November 1567 an act of the Privy Council refers to the habit of the thieves of Liddesdale of holding people to ransom. The Privy Council states 'that many persons are content to pay blackmail to these thieves and sit under their protection permitting them to reave, harry, and oppress their neighbours in their sight without contradiction or stop'. The Privy Council forbade such practices under pain of heavy penalties and stated that, 'when any companies of thieves or broken men comes over the valleys within the in-country, all dwelling in the bounds shall incontinent cry on hie, raise the fray, and follow them, as well in their in-passing as out-passing, in order to get back the stolen goods or beasts'.

In an attempt to subdue the border reivers, the governments on both sides of the border divided the region for administrative purposes into six areas known as the Marches, three on the Scottish side and three on the English. Each of the six Marches had a governing officer known as a Warden, appointed by the respective governments. The raiding season was generally autumn to spring, when the cattle and their owners were in their permanent winter quarters in the valleys, although Sir Robert Carey, Warden of the Middle March, pronounced the last months of the year as the worst, 'for then are the nights longest, their horses at hard meat, and will ride best, cattle strong, and will drive farthest'. They commonly rode in family parties

Highland soldiers wearing the belted plaid.
Radio Times Hulton Picture Library

– Liddesdale raids were almost always made up of Elliots, Armstrongs, Crosers and Nixons, just as the Redesdale and Tynedale incursions consisted largely of Charltons, Dodds, Milburns and Robsons.

Raids varied in size. Bands of a dozen to fifty riders were normal and great forays in which upwards of two or three thousand reivers took part. The objectives varied from the theft of a single animal to a raid on an entire town or even several towns. Border raids are recorded within three miles of Edinburgh and as far south as Yorkshire. Bishop Leslie writes:

> They sally out of their own Borders in the night in troops, through unfrequented byways and many intricate windings. All the daytime they refresh themselves and their horses in lurking places they have pitched upon before, till they arrive in the dark at those places they have a design upon. As soon as they have seized upon

the booty, they in like manner, return home in the night through blind ways, fetching many a compass. The more skilful any captain is to pass through those wild deserts, crooked turnings, and deep precipices, in the thickest mists and darkness, his reputation is the greater and he is looked upon as a man of excellent head.

Family unity as much as anything made the Borders and set them apart. Despite the feudal system, tribal loyalty was paramount. Feuds were frequent, and often lasted generations. The bitterest quarrel, which lasted four centuries, was between the Maxwells and the Johnsons, who were rivals for the wardenship of the area. The Lowlands families also occupied distinct areas. Galloway was dominated by the Kennedys and the Maxwells and Hamilton occupied much of Strathclyde. In the eastern Lowlands, the Homes lived in Berwickshire, and the Kerrs, Scotts and Hepburns on the Border. The great family of Mackintosh, occupied much of Moray and Inverness-shire, the Gordons extended through Mar and Buchan and the Ogilvys were mainly found in Angus. Like the Highlanders, the Marchmen at their own sense of community strengthened by inter-marriage and blood kinship.

This strong sense of a common heritage united Scots and English clans on both sides of the Border which was frowned upon by the authorities in England and Scotland. During Somerset's expedition into Scotland in the middle of the sixteenth century when the opposing forces met it was noted that each was seen talking to each other 'within less than a spear's length, but when aware that such intercourse was noticed, they commenced to run at each other, apparently with no desire to inflict serious injury.' 'There is too great familiarity and intercourse between our England and Scottish borders' Sir John Carey, Warden of the Middle March, complained to the Privy Council 'the gentlemen of both counties crossing into either at their pleasure, feasting and making merry with their friends, overthrowing the Wardens' authority and all Border law'.

It was not until the accession of James VI of Scotland to the English throne in 1603 that the borders finally came under government control. James was determined to obliterate all barriers between England and Scotland. It was his intention that 'the very heart of the country shall not be left in an uncertainty'. The laws and usages of the borders and marches were now 'vanished and delete'. The Border no longer existed; where the old Marches had been would now be 'The Middle Shires'. In 1605 James formed a single commission of five Englishmen to control the entire Border region on both sides. There followed a period of intensive and ruthless government such as the region had never known. In 1606 a number of English Grahams, one of the more troublesome English Border families, were transported to Connaught while thirty-two Borderers were executed and 300, Armstrongs, Elliots, Johnstones, Kerrs, Irvines and Nixons included, were declared official fugitives.

Gradually the old Border was subdued. From north and south the royal lieutenants attacked the Border keeps and broke the military power strongholds of the barons. The greater lords from the borders became courtiers; the lesser nobles and their families led peaceable lives as rural lairds. In July 1609 a mass hanging of thieves taken by Cranston was held at Dumfries and the Chancellor Dunfermline was able to report that the Earl 'has purgit the Borders of all the chiefest malefactors, robbers and brigands...as Hercules sometimes is written to have purged Augeas the King of Elides his escuries'. The Middle Shires, Dunfermline concluded were now 'as quiet as any part in any civil kingdom in Christeanity'.

Many of the old riding clans saw the end to their way of life and chose exile rather than submission. In 1603 about 2000 Scots crossed with Walter Scott of Buccleuch to the Low Countries to help the States in their war against Spain. When the Spanish Ambassador in London complained he was told that King James was 'not altogether displeased that this rabble should be taken out of the Kingdom'. Many of those who had been outlawed by the Border Commission fled to the Plantation in Ulster. They frequently took with them cattle and horses stolen in the Lowlands or Borders, which met with a ready sale on the Irish side of the channel where they were much in demand by the new settlers.

Meanwhile in the Highlands, life went on much as it had for five hundred years or more. What happened in Edinburgh or in the Anglicized Lowlands had very little relevance. Here a different system, different loyalties and standards prevailed largely in defiance of church and state. The clan system was based on the ownership of land which was vested in the chief of the clan, though there was much overlapping of clan territory which led to disputes and fights between the clans. Feuds were a frequent feature of Highland life. One of the most memorable was that between clans Chattan and Kay. On 28 September 1396, thirty men from each clan lined up in a purpose-built enclosure on the north Inch of Perth. King Robert III and several members of his court lined up to watch the slaughter. The men of

Portrait of Prince Charles Edward Stuart, 1732, by Antonio David. Scottish National Portrait Gallery

Clan Chattan, finding themselves one short as battle commenced, persuaded 'a gallant saddler of Perth to volunteer his services for half a French gold dollar'. By the time the King ended the contest, 29 Kays were dead, the one survivor swimming to safety across the Tay, while only ten of Clan Chattan and the saddler had survived.

The land, once held by the tribe in common, had by the eighteenth century becomes the chief's, his title to it sometimes no more tangible than the approval of his tribe. Part of it was 'mensal land' used by and for the chief himself. Parts, too, might be given in perpetuity to families of officials of the clan, men like the Bard, the Harper and the Piper. The rest was held by tenants under 'tacks' or leases granted by the chief. Reiving, or the *creach* had been for centuries a rite of passage when young men took livestock from neighbouring clans. By the seventeenth century this had declined and most reiving was the *spreidh* where up to ten men raided the adjoining Lowlands, the livestock taken usually being recoverable on payment of *tascal* (information money) and guarantee of no prosecution. Some clans offered the Lowlanders protection against such raids, on terms not dissimilar to blackmail.

The chief protected the clan and the chief punished the clan. Sometimes offenders were driven from the glens, on other occasions they might be sold to the merchant captains who called at Inverness, looking for servants for the Americas. Seven years before Culloden, Sir Alexander Macdonald of Sleat and his brother-in-law Macleod of Dunvegan, chiefs of the Isles, drove one hundred of their people aboard ships for deportation to Pennsylvania, and survived the uproar this caused in the Lowlands when the ship was discovered and the deportees released at an Irish port. Englishman Edward Burt went to the Highlands early in the eighteenth century to help Marshal Wade build military roads in the region left an account of his meeting with a Highland chief: 'I happened to be at the house of a certain chief, when the chieftain of another tribe came to make a visit. I told him I thought some of his people had not behaved towards me with that civility I expected of the clan. He started, clapped his hand on his broadsword and said, if I required it, he would send me two or three of their heads. I laughed, thinking it a joke, but the chief insisted he was a man of his word'.

The Highlands had no written history, and a man's reputation and memory depended on the skill of the Bard. He was also the clan's principal genealogist. 'They had a pride in their family', said Burt, 'almost everyone is a genealogist.' Burt had an Englishman's contempt for such pride in family history: 'This kind of vanity...in people of no fortune, makes them ridiculous...Thus you see a gentleman may be a mercenary piper, or keep a little ale-house where be brews his drink in a kettle; but to be of any working trade would be a disgrace to him, his present relations and all his ancestry...'

Although the Highland clans are often seen as the ancient representatives of Gaelic Scotland, the origins of the clans is surprising complex with Celtic, Pictish, Viking and Norman ancestors claimed by various Highland chiefs. Some clans such as Clan Campbell and Clan Donald claimed ancient Celtic mythological progenitors mentioned in the ancient Irish Fenian cycle, a body of prose and verse centering on the exploits of the mythical hero Fionn mac Cumhaill and his warriors the Fianna Éireann. Another group including Clan MacSween, Clan Lamont, Clan MacEwen of Otter, Clan Maclachlan, and MacNeil tracing their ancestry back to the fifth century High King of Ireland. Others such as Clan MacAulay, Clan Mackinnon and Clan Gregor claim descent from the Scots King Kenneth Mac Alpin who made himself King of the Picts in AD 843.

The Macleods, established on the mainland below the Kyle of Lochalsh, were of Norse origin, being descended from Magnus, the last king of the

The Last of the Clan by Thomas Faed. Glasgow Art Gallery & Museum

Isle of Man. Similarly the Gunns and the MacLeods were of Viking blood; the Campbells and Galbraiths descend from ancient Britons of the old Kingdom of Strathclyde. The Leslies traced their descent back to Bartolf of Hungary, who came over with Queen Margaret. Families of Norman origin such as the Chisholms, who finally settled in Strath Glass, the Cummings, above Loch Ericht, the Frasers, encircling the north of Loch Ness, the Gordons, surrounding Huntly and the Stewarts spreading below Perth were examples of Norman barons granted, or acquiring through marriage or by other means, estates in the north around which eventually a clan formed.

Both Clans Campbell and Donald provide outstanding examples of shifting fortunes. From Strathclyde, the Campbells married into an early Argyllshire dynasty and by supporting Robert I launched themselves on a steady political climb which culminated in their becoming the most powerful clan in the country by the seventheenth century. This was largely at the expense of the Clan Donald, who as Lords of the Isles, dominated the west Highlands and Island for over 150 years. Unlike the Campbells they preferred to defy the Scottish Crown and at one time their power was almost equal to that of the Scottish king. Eventually their power was broken and their territory dwindled to include Kintyre, the Isle of Slay, parts of Skye and parts of the mainland including Ardnamurchan and Glencoe.

It is a common assumption that clans were formed by people all bearing the same surname. Duncan Forbes, Lord President of the Court of Session, left an account of the clans in the mid-eighteenth century: 'A Highland Clan', he wrote, 'is a set of men all bearing the same surname, and believing themselves to be related the one to the other, and to be descended from the same common stock. In each clan there are several subaltern tribes, who own their dependence on their own immediate chiefs but all agree in owing allegiance to the Supreme Chief of the Clan or Kindred and look upon it to be their duty to support him at all adventures.' It fact until the seventeenth century few Highlanders had surnames at all. A clan consisted of men bearing a great variety of names. When surnames came into use in the Highlands many of the clansmen adopted the surname of their chief.

By the sixteenth century more and more the legal possession of land became the main factor in Highland disputes. In 1578 at Trumpan, Isle of Skye, a marauding force of MacDonalds of Uist locked the door of the church on a congregation of MacLeods and set fire to the thatched roof. Only one girl managed to escape to raise the alarm. The chief of the MacLeods led a force out of Dunvegan Castle, intercepted the departing MacDonalds in Ardmore Bay, and massacred them in revenge. Meanwhile large clan battles continued. In 1598 at the Battle of Gruinart in Islay, between the MacLeans of Duart and the MacDonalds of Dunyvaig, 280 MacLeans were killed and at the Battle of Glen Fruin in 1603 the MacGregors slaughtered 180 Colquhouns and suffered only two loses. The chief Alasdair MacGregor, was captured and hanged, and all the MacGregors who fought at Glen Fruin were outlawed.

The Stewart Kings were frequently exasperated by the outrages commited by the clans and their determination to flout their ambition to make Scotland a peaceful and well ordered kingdom. At various times the Stuarts banished or destroyed clans that had become nuisances. They destroyed the Clan Donald's power in the western Highlands and islands, and handed over its lands to the Campbells. They did the same to the Clan Leod of Lewis, and the MacIains of Ardnamurchan. James V was dissatisfied with the standard of law and order in the Highlands and responded by issuing 'Letters of Fire and Sword' to his half-brother James, Earl of Moray, and several other chiefs, authorizing them to destroy the Clan Chattan with the exception of its women, priests and children, who were to be deported and set ashore on the coasts of Shetland and Norway. Fortunately for the Clan Chattan his commission was not carried out effectively.

The problem of the MacGregor clan, relatively small, close-knit and fiercely independent, was that they had no charter to their ancestral grounds. Caught between Campbell of Argyll and Campbell of Breadalbane, they had the status of squatters. They were treated as thieves, outlawed, their name was banned and they were subjected to savage harassment. The 'wicked and unhappy race of the Clan Gregour' as the Register of the Privy Council described it, would have been extinguished had in not given shelter by other clans.

The real winner in the destruction of the MacGregors was Clan Campbell which moved in and occupied their former territory. In fact, the Campbells and their most important chiefs, the Dukes of Argyll, rose to power by serving as the Crown's principal tool in controlling the western clans. This reached its climax when the newly crowned William III offered a pardon to those Highland clans for their part in the Jacobite Uprising, provided they took an oath of allegiance before 1 January 1692. The MacDonalds of Glencoe missed the deadline and in late January or early February 1692, the first and second companies of the Earl of Argyll's Regiment of Foot, around 120 men, under the command of Captain Robert Campbell arrived at Glencoe where they were received in the hospitable tradition of the Highlands. On 13 February 1692, the regiment finally received instructions:

> You are hereby ordered to fall upon the Rebels, the McDonalds of Glencoe, and putt all to the sword under seventy. you are to have a special care that the old Fox and his sons doe upon no account escape your hands, you are to secure all the avenues that no man escape. This you are to putt in execution at fyve of the clock precisely; and by that time, or very shortly after it, I'll strive to be att you with a stronger party: if I doe not come to you att fyve, you are not to tarry for me, but to fall on. This is by the Kings speciall command, for the good & safty of the Country, that these miscreants be cutt off root and branch.

At five the following morning the troops butchered at least thirty-five of their hosts. The elderly chief, Iain MacIain was shot in the back while he was rising from his bed to dress.

By the eighteenth century the power of the clans had been broken. It is ironic therefore that the national dress of Scotland should become that which was until the nineteenth century most closely associated with the Highland clans: the wearing of tartan. About 1695 Martin Martin, born on Skye, wrote a book entitled *A Description of the Western Isles of Scotland*, which gives a reasonably clear idea of the development of Highland dress and the tartans worn at the turn of the seventeenth century. He wrote:

> The Plaid worn by the Men, is made of fine Wool, the Thread as fine as can be made of that kind; it consists of divers Colours... Every Isle differs from each other... tho the main Land of the Highlands, in-so-far that they who have seen these Places, are able at the first view of a man's Plaid, to guess the place of his residence...

This is the first mention of the difference in setts, or patterns, of tartans as varying in different localities. It seems likely that each glen would have its favourite vegetable dyes, which predominated locally, and these would be most commonly used in that area.

The clan tartan did not exist during the heyday of clan warfare: the clansman identified himself by wearing a sprig of his clan's chosen plant pinned to his bonnet. The Campbells, for example, wore the wild myrtle, the

Sir Walter Scott in 1823 by Andrew Geddes. The National Portrait Gallery

Gordons ivy and the MacKenzies holly. Up to the sixteenth century most clansmen had probably gone bare-headed, but the Lowland blue bonnet was then adopted as the universal headwear of the Highlands.

Following the Union of 1707 tartan began to be worn was a nationalist symbol: Lowland lairds and their wives and children were portrayed sporting tartan to signify their anti-Union principles.

The association of tartan with rebellion led to the proscription of Highland dress in 1746. When the Act was finally rescinded in the late eighteenth century, visitors to the Highlands noted that the traditional dress was not readopted by the ordinary Highlander.

Doctor Johnson noted that 'the same poverty that made it then difficult for them to change their clothing, hinders them now from changing it again'. . In the later nineteenth century when George Washington Wilson, David Octavious Hill and other pioneering photographers recorded scenes of Highland life, there as little tartan to be seen. In these pictures the Highland poor are dressed in clothes of Lowland style, in tweed, serge and flannel. Highland dress had become the costume of the aristocracy and gentry, when they chose to war it, and of the prosperous middle class who increasingly visited the Highlands and acquired property there.

The visit of King George IV to Scotland in 1822 had a great deal to do with the adoption by all Scots of tartan as part of the national dress. The peers of Scotland, and more particular chief organiser of the event Sir Walter Scott, proposed to entertain his Majesty with a Grand Ball at the Assembly Rooms in George Street, Edinburgh. Sir Walter Scott reminded his readers that Mr Hunter was 'preparing a magnificent dress of the royal tartan for His Majesty' to wear and said that everyone who has seen the King must now 'be anxious to contemplate his fine person in his noblest of all British costumes'. There was one unalterable condition upon which admission to the Assembly Rooms depended. With the exception of those in uniform, 'no Gentleman is to be allowed to appear in any thing but the ancient Highland costume'. This resulted in a great many new tartans being established since those clan chiefs who could not decide upon a single pattern could always find a tailor to invent one for them. Others adapted a regimental tartan associated with a particular clan or area.

If a single occasion can be said to have determined the kilt as the national dress of all Scotsmen this Ball many perhaps have been that moment. The enthusiasm for Gaelic culture led to the formation of the Highland Societies of Edinburgh, Inverness, Aberdeen, London and elsewhere. The Highland

Society of Edinburgh was formed in 1784, its founding members were all Highland proprietors many of whom were driving the Highland population from their estates and replacing them with sheep. The Highland Society of Aberdeen declared that it first objects was to 'promote the general use of the ancient Highland dresses. All members were obliged to attend meetings in Highland clothes of their own tartan. The Highland Society in London professed the same objects. Stewart of Garth, who joined the London Society in 1815, moved a resolution which 'was highly approved and applauded' which proposed a register of clan tartans, for which 'the Chiefs of the Clans should be requested to furnish a specimen of their Clan Tartan, properly authenticated and signed and certificated by their signature and Family Arms'. It is from this point that tartans became associated with a particular clan or family.

One achievement of the cultivation by Lowlanders of clans and tartans has been to efface the old distinctions between Highlands and Lowlands, which had already broken down with migration and intermarriage. The tartan industry today forms a significant part of the overall textiles sector in Scotland and comprises weavers, textile merchants and manufacturers and makers of kilts, tartans and accessories. An economic impact study of the tartan industry in Scotland, commissioned by Scottish Enterprise in 2007, showed the tartan industry contributes some £350m to the Scottish economy and supporting 3,000 direct and 4,000 indirect jobs. Highland dress, which only two centuries earlier was in danger of being relegated to the pages of history, has now come to symbolise more than anything else the wearers pride in his Scottish ancestry.

Chapter Five

EDUCATION

Education has always been considered very important by Scots: indeed, Scotland's first Education Act was passed as far back as 1496, when James IV ordered that the eldest sons of barons and free-holders should study Latin, arts and law, in order to ensure that local government lay in knowledgeable hands. Two hundred years later a further education act ordered that a school be established in every parish, and by the end of the eighteenth century Scotland's literacy rate would be higher than that of any other country in Europe. In the early nineteenth century English economist Thomas Malthus had no doubts about the benefits this education system had wrought on the Scottish working-class: 'The knowledge circulated among the common people…has yet the effect of making them bear with patience the evils which they suffer from, being aware of the folly and inefficacy of turbulence. The quiet and peaceable habits of the instructed Scotch peasant compared with the turbulent disposition of the ignorant Irishman ought not to be without effect upon every impartial reasoner.'

Before the Reformation there were two kinds of school in Scotland. The first was the lecture school, where children were taught in the vernacular. The higher category of school was the grammar school, where pupils were taught Latin, and the humanities generally. The Latin teaching schools were usually attached to the monasteries, or were situated in the royal burghs. Most of the principal towns in Scotland boasted grammar schools which were under the control of the church. The most outstanding grammar schools were those of Glasgow, Dunfermline, Perth, Stirling, Linlithgow, and Dundee. The teaching in the Catholic grammar schools naturally favoured Latin and subjects connected with religion. Other schools existed, but proof that the authorities favoured the grammar schools was shown in

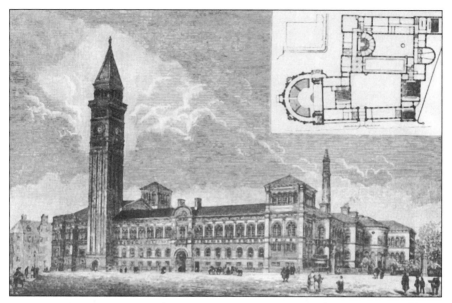

University Medical School. From James Grant, Old & New Edinburgh, *issued in weekly instalments c.1890.*

1520 by Edinburgh Town Council which enacted 'that no inhabitant of the town should put their children to any school in the burgh but to the principal grammar school to be taught in any science except only grace book, primer, and plain duty under a fine of 10s'.

After the Reformation, the church retained its control over education. The *First Book of Discipline* in 1560 set out an ambitious plan to have elementary schools in every parish, grammar schools in every town, high schools or colleges in every large town and provision for the university study of arts, medicine, law and divinity. The scheme was to be for the good of society as a whole 'sa that the commonwealthe many have some comfort bythem', but this ideal that was too advanced for the Scottish Parliament at the time. James Melville, nephew of the famous Presbyterian reformer Andrew Melville, left an entertaining account of his school days at Montrose in the 1560s:

> There we learned to read the Catechism, Prayers and Scripture; to rehearse the Catechism and prayers par coeur; also make notes of

Scripture after the reading thereof; and there first I found (blessed be my Good God for it!) that spirit of sanctification beginning to work some motions in my heart, een about the eighth or ninth year of my age; to pray going to bed and rising, and being in the fields alone to say over the prayers with a sweet moving of my heart and to abhor swearing...We learned the rudiments of the Latin grammar with the vocalbularies in Latin and Frenchl also divers speeches in French with the reading and right pronuication of the tongue...

It is clear from Melville's account that the boys received a good all round education which still left room for sport and leisure:

There we also had the air good and fields reasonably far, and by our master were taught to handle the bow for archery, the club for golf, the batons for fencing, also to run, to leap, to swim, to wrestle, to practise all exploits by everyone having his match and antagonist – both in our lessons and play.

At the end of the sixteenth century a Royal Commission was set up under George Buchanan and Peter Young, the tutors of the young King James VI.

Adam Smith. From John Kay, A Series of Original Portraits, With Biographical Sketches and Illustrative Anecdotes. Edinburgh, A C Black, 1877

The Commission included the headmasters of the grammar schools at Edinburgh, Stirling, Dunbar, Haddington, Glasgow and St Andrews. It was decided that the school books were not up to the required standard, and consequently a new grammar was ordered to be written. By 1593 this had been done, and the Privy Council ordered the new grammar to be proclaimed at all the market crosses, and afterwards it was ordered to be in general use all over Scotland:

> Forasmuch as it is understood by the King's Majesty and Lords of Secret Council that the masters of schools and pedagogues have this many years bygone chosen to themselves such writings of the arts of grammar as have been commended unto them by booksellers, which they have learned themselves or else been accustomed to teach, or such as upon the occasion of the time, and place come readiest to their hands; whereby it often comes to pass that the best and most profitable form for advancing of the studies of the youth has not been taught, both such as they find to be most easy for sparing and retaining their work, and likewise thee by many and diverse grammars are brought in and taught in the country as there are teachers of that art; so that when scholars changed from place to place at the arbitrement of their parents they are newlings to being that art where they have spent some years before, and are rather charged there to forget, nor repeat that which they have learned, to the great hindering of their proceedings and the confounding of their memories and intelligence.

In spite of the ambitious plans of the Reformers, it is clear that Scottish education in the early seventeenth century that much needed to be done to improve the standard of educational provision in the country. The Commissioners' Report on the State of Parishes in 1627 bore striking evidence that most of the reported parishes were without a school, a schoolmaster, or any means of maintaining one. According to the returns of eight parishes in Berwickshire, with about 2,500 communicants, not one has a school – though the Commissioners urged that 'a schoole is great neede', 'most necessary by a multitude of poor common people;' and of Mordington it said 'none can wryt or reid except the minister'.

In many places the kirk was used as a schoolroom; in others the church steeple, a family vault, a granary, a byre or stable or any other dilapidated hovel was utilised. In many cases there were no desks to write at and no benches to sit upon, and the scholars lay on floors. Thomas Kirk, when he travelled from Yorkshire to Scotland in 1677, was amazed at the state of the school at Burntisland, where there was no stool or form, and only a seat for the master. The children sat on the earth floor in a litter on the heather and grass with which the grown as strewn 'like pigs in a stye'.

During the seventeenth century there was a moderate but steady expansion of both parish and burgh schools. These efforts culminated in an Act of 1696 which, with some amendments in 1803 and later years, remained the basis of Scottish educational legislation down to 1872. The 'heritors' in each parish (the substantial landowners) were obliged to maintain a school, open to boys and girls alike, and to appoint a salaried schoolmaster. The funds were provided by a rate on landed property, the minister exercised day-to-day supervision, and the presbyteries of the Church inspected the schools and tested the teachers' religious and scholarly qualifications. The teachers were expected to teach the Church's 'Shorter Catechism', but their main business was to teach reading and writing to all. Some parish schoolmasters were also expected to teach the so-called 'university subjects' – Latin, mathematics, and perhaps Greek – the universities admitting boys at fifteen or even younger providing elementary instruction in the 'junior classes' which began the college course. For boys with talent but no resources, bursaries for university study were widely available, and many of these impecunious students would return to the parishes and burghs as schoolmasters.

Scottish schoolmasters in the seventeenth and eighteenth centuries were poorly paid, if they were paid at all, depending as they were upon reluctant local heritors or an impoverished church to pay their wages. Many faced a life of considerable hardship. In 1748 they framed a memorial to be presented to the General Assembly and to Parliament appealing for improved pay and conditions. 'It is certain', stated the petition, 'that our present encouragement will not procure even the necessities of life to any person, though he should live at the lowest rate, being only at an average of about £11 sterling, or about 7d. a day, which is less than the lowest mechanic can earn'.

They made little progress and were too poor to prosecute their cause for long. Instead they were often dependent upon 'gifts' such as candles at Candlemas and one penny from each scholar on the first Mondays of May, June and July. These were holidays called 'bent silver days' the money being

High School of 1578, William Steven, The History of the High School of Edinburgh. Edinburgh, 1849

nominally to buy the 'bent' or rushes to cover the earthen floor of the schoolroom, but really was devoted to buying clothes for the master's ragged family. There was also the peat brought by each scholar in the morning for the fire in winter, if the school was luxurious enough to have a hearth fire at all.

For the pupils, school began as soon as light would permit. In rural parishes they met from October to February at sunrise and were dismissed at sunset, while during the rest of the year they attended from seven in the morning till six in the evening, with two hours' interval for breakfast and dinner. In 1737, for example, rules were laid down by the Presbytery that the school of Inverurie shall be open from the time scholars can see to read in the morning till twelve o'clock noon, and from one o'clock till the light fail at night, from November till February, and thereafter from eight o'clock in the morning till six.

Holidays during the pre-Reformation period were fairly numerous owing to the many saints in the calendar, but with the advent of the Reformation holidays and festivals were frowned upon. Needless to say, the boys did not share in this feeling, and they frequently struck against the loss of their privileges. It was apparently an old custom at Aberdeen Grammar School that for two weeks at Christmas the pupils took possession of the school 'to the exclusion of their masters and all authority'. Despite efforts by local magistrates to end this custom, 'school disorder' broke out in December 1647 when 'the boys keeping and holding the school against their masters with swords, guns, pistols, and other weapons, spulying [despoiling] and taking of poor folks gear, such as geese, fowls, peats [magpies] and other vivres during the holding thereof'. The magistrates ordered that to avoid 'such disorders in future no boy from without the town shall be admitted without a caution for his good behaviour'.

Little information is available concerning discipline in Scottish schools at this time. One master was instructed to punish 'as he may think fit,' another is to do so 'according to the quality of the fault' or 'at his discretion.' Swearing, Sabbath-breaking, and rebellious disobedience were to be punished for the first offence by public whipping, for the second by flogging, and for the third by expulsion from the school. In the early eighteenth century the Town Council of Dunbar took the enlightened attitude that the rod should be spared as long as possible, but when admonition, warning, and threats fail, the master was not to 'spare the child for his much crying.'

By the early part of the nineteenth century, the Lowland countryside was well served with a single school in each parish. Supervision by the Church of Scotland presbyteries ensured that a high proportion of the population achieved basic literary skills. In the Reminiscences of Dr Findlater, who is remembered as the editor of *Chambers' Encyclopaedia*, we have a description of the parish school in Aberdeenshire in which he was taught, in the first quarter of the nineteenth century:

The dimensions were 34 by 14, and the height of the side walls 6 feet. A portion of the room was partitioned off, along each side stood a long flat table or desk with a form attached to each side, so that the scholars sat facing each other. A considerable space was thus left vacant in the middle of the floor, and there stood the master's chair without any desk. The fire burned on an open hearth : there was no flue, the smoke issuing by the usual lum (chimney). A part of the school-room space was taken up with a pile of peats. This store was kept up by each scholar bringing a peat every morning under his arm … The floor was of earth, and usually well worn into holes. The duty of removing the ashes, kindling the fire, and sweeping the floor devolved on a censor appointed weekly. The sweeping was mostly confined to the middle of the floor. The dust under the desks was rarely disturbed, and generally lay about an inch deep … I do not think that I ever heard Mr Craik (the schoolmaster) ask the meaning of a word or sentence, or offer to explain the one or the other … In the curriculum of the Aberdour School neither grammar, history nor geography formed a part.

The parish school legislation did not apply to towns, and although by custom all burghs were expected to maintain a burgh school, these often hardly rose above the level of a parish school, and only in the largest towns did burgh schools give an education of a mainly secondary type. In the burgh schools pupils received a course lasting about four years – longer in the larger schools, like Glasgow, where it was lengthened in 1815 to five years, and Edinburgh where it might stretch to six or seven. They entered at the age of nine or ten, having mastered their letters in the English school. By 1868 there were fifty-four burgh schools in Scotland, of which twenty-one were partly run by the heritors of the local parish, the rest entirely by the town council.

The importance of an education to even the lowest classes of society in Scotland was noted in 1796: 'even day-labourers give their children a good education … an important advantage which the Scots as a nation enjoy over the natives of other countries'. But it was also observed that 'the want of proper schoolmasters' accounted for much of the ignorance and bigotry which was alleged to prevail in many parts of the country. An Act of 1803 was designed to improve matters by laying down improved standards of salary and housing for schoolmasters imposing more stringent obligations upon heritors to make provisions for them. The Act may be seen as the beginning of state control of education in Scotland

The attention paid by both the Church and state to education in Scotland ensured that the country became Europe's first modern literate society. This meant that there was an audience not only for the Bible but for other books as well. Even a person of relatively modern means had his own collection of books, and what he could not afford he could get at the local lending library, which by 1750 virtually every town of any size enjoyed. A good example is

Innerpeffray, near Crieff in Perthshire. Its library's record of book borrowing runs from 1747 to 1800. They show books loaned out to the local baker, the blacksmith, the cooper, the dyer and the dyer's apprentice and to farmers, stonemasons, quarries, tailors and household servants.

Robert Burns's father was a poor farmer from Alloway in south-western Scotland, who had taught his son to make a living by handling a plough. But he also saw to it that young Robert received an education worthy of any English gentleman, including studying Latin and French. 'Though I cost the schoolmaster some thrashings', Burns remembered later, 'I made an excellent scholar'. The first books he read were a biography of Hannibal and *The Life of Sir William Wallace*, lent to him by the local blacksmith. 'The story of Wallace poured a Scottish prejudice in my views', Burns recalled, 'which will boil along there till the flood gates of life shut in eternal rest'.

In Edinburgh the book trade was an important part of the local economy. By 1790 there were sixteen publishing houses for a population of just over 60,000. Papermaking became a mainstay of the national economy. The paper mill was often the only industry in rural villages and hamlets in the Lowlands agricultural belt. The one at Currie brought 200 new inhabitants into the village when it opened. An official national survey in 1795 showed that out of a population of 1.5 million, nearly 20,000 Scots depended for their livelihood on writing and publishing – and 10,500 on teaching.

At the highest level of the educational system, all five universities managed to survive the violent seventeenth century. The three papal foundations of the middle ages, St Andrews, Glasgow and King's College, Old Aberdeen, and the two post-medieval and secular institutions, Edinburgh and Marischal College, in New Aberdeen. Glasgow and St Andrews enjoyed a long reputation that reached back to the Middle Ages. The greatest figure of later medieval thought, John Duns Scotus, had been a Scot, while John Muir, dubbed 'the prince of philosophers and theologians' at the University of Paris, finished his career teaching at both Glasgow and St Andrews (where his students included George Buchanan and John Knox). In 1574 an observer wrote that 'there is no place in Europe comparable to Glasgow for a plentiful and gude chepe mercat of all kind of langages artes and sciences'.

The University of Edinburgh and Aberdeen's Marischal College and King's College were later foundations, but, like Glasgow and St Andrews, they never became remote ivory towers or intellectual backwaters, as eighteenth-century Oxford and Cambridge did. Despite their small size, Scottish universities were international centres of learning, and drew students from across Protestant Europe as well as England and Ulster (since only Episcopalians could attend Oxford or Cambridge or Trinity College in Dublin). Edinburgh differed from the others in that it was not an independent university but a 'toun's college'. The town council appointed and dismissed the teachers, paid their salaries, and regulated students' fees and courses of study.

At Glasgow the tuition fee of £5 a year was one-tenth the cost of going to Cambridge or Oxford. A father in trade, commerce or the professions was more typical than a working- or labouring-class one; but even this contrasted with the socially top-heavy landed gentry and aristocratic student bodies in the English universities. More than half of the students at the University of Glasgow between 1740 and 1830 came from middle-class backgrounds. Most of the students lived in bare and comfortless college chambers, though a few wealthier boys boarded with the regents or in private houses with 'masters', who might give them extra-mural tuition. Gowns were worn not only in college but also on the public streets. Speech, even informal conversation, was allowed only in Latin. St Andrews was the

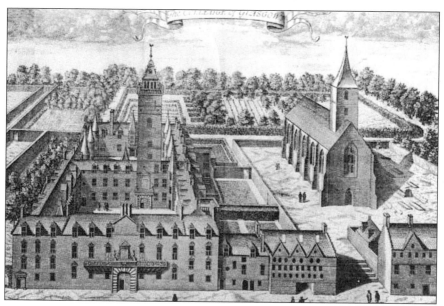

The College of Glasgow, from John Slezer's Theatrum Scotiae, 1693.

fashionable university and attracted the sons of nobles as well as of lairds and merchants. But the great majority of the boys at the Scottish universities took the 'Arts' or 'Philosophy' course with a view to the ministry.

Attending university classes also became a favourite hobby among Edinburgh and Aberdeen townspeople, just as professors regularly engaged in a 'community outreach' to offer classes to students outside the academic setting. Robert Dick, at the University of Glasgow, taught natural philosophy to a lecture hall of townspeople, men and women, in the 1750s. In the early nineteenth century, University of Edinburgh chemistry professor Thomas Hope's public lectures drew more than three hundred ladies from the town. It is clear that for Scots at all levels of society, education had become a way of life.

Things were very different in the Scottish Highlands. It was not until after the rebellion of 1715 that Parliament directed its attention to the condition of the Highlands. King George I recognised that poverty and illiteracy in the Highlands constituted a menace to his throne, and in 1721 he persuaded Parliament to vote for the support of schools in the Highlands a grant of £20,000 from the sale of Scottish estates forfeited after the rebellion. How much of this money ever reached the Highlands is very debatable. However, changes for the better were already underway with the founding of the Society for Propagating Christian Knowledge. In 1701 a few private gentlemen met in Edinburgh and established a society for the purpose of 'further promoting Christian knowledge and the increase of piety and virtue within Scotland, especially in the Highlands, Islands, and remote corners thereof.' They saw the education of the young as there first task and proceeded to set up schools for teaching reading, writing, arithmetic, and the elements of Christian knowledge.

The Society from the outset had the support of the General Assembly, and letters patent were received from Queen Anne erecting it into a corporation with considerable powers and privileges. Its capital, which in 1706 was £1000, had risen in 1781 to £34,000, and by that year it had under its control 180 schools with an attendance of 7000 scholars. Initially the Society took the attitude that the Gaelic language was the cause of the backwardness of the Highlands, and the directors insisted that all instruction should be given in English. This policy was reversed in 1767, and in 1781 the directors report that the change, far from interfering with the progress in English, had resulted in an increased interest in it and a more intelligent knowledge of it. Encouraged by this progress the Society had the New Testament translated into Gaelic, in 1768 and widely distributed throughout the Highlands. The policy was continued throughout the nineteenth century when the Gaelic-speaking Highlanders had an unexpected advocate in Queen Victoria, who insisted that Highland children should be educated through the medium of their own language. In 1849 she communicated her ideas to Lord Lansdowne, one of her Ministers '...it is really a great mistake that the people should be constantly taking a language which they often can not read and generally not write'. In his reply, Lord Lansdowne undertook '...to combine instruction in the Gaelic with the English language...and to have a view to it in the choice of inspectors.'

Meanwhile in the growing industrial cities of the Scottish Lowlands the burgh grammar schools simply could not cope with the rapidly increasing populations. Nearly two-thirds of all the schoolchildren in Scotland in 1818 were found to be outside these public institutions and mainly in small private schools known as 'adventure' schools where parents bore all the costs and in which the Church has no say. By the 1820s a crusade to supplement the parochial schools with Church 'sessional' and 'General Assembly' schools in the towns attracted generous donations from the congregations, greatly assisted by public finance after 1834, when the Government began to give grants to schools in Scotland. This work was supplemented after the Disruption in 1843, by the Free Church which initially set up many hundreds of its own schools to supplement and rival those of the Church of Scotland. It soon found the strain on its funds to be such that it could not cope without government grants and government inspection. The United Presbyterians were a third force in local education and, the increasing bands of Irish Catholics in the towns and cities of the Lowlands led to the direct involvement of the Catholic Church in the education of its parishioners.

The biggest problem faced by all of these groups in the industrial towns was the increasing demand for child labour. According to Robert Somers, in Glasgow in 1857, under half the population aged between five and ten was attending school at all: 'Every branch of skilled labour as well as our shops and warehouses, offer employment to little boys who can read and scrawl their names. For a still less educated class, there are the factories, the bleachfields, the tobacco-works and a host of minor manufactures. Making matches, stringing beads or bugles on ladies' dresses, and a hundred other trivial occupations, absorb the labour of multitudes of children of both sexes, irrespective almost of age and totally irrespective of their instruction'.

Glashmore School, a Kirk Session School. From The History of Scottish Education by James Scotland.

By the middle of the nineteenth century the exploitation of children in factories was gradually eliminated. Althorp's Act of 1833, laid down a minimum age for the employment of children in cotton mills of nine years, limited their hours to eight in the day up to the age of thirteen, and appointed inspectors: in Scotland the effects were seriously undermined by the absence of civil registration until 1855. The Mines Act of 1842 prohibited the labour of women and young children below ground, and thereby ended the horrible system by which boys of seven or eight worked in darkness and filth drawing tubs of coal from the face for fourteen hours a day. Ironically as industrial expansion increased, more children were employed. The Argyll Commission, discovering in 1867 that one-fifth of children of school age were not receiving education, attributed it partly to the fact that 'child labour abounded wherever the Factory Act is not in operation.'

To deal with this problem the state took an increasing role in the education system. Grants were made for education in 1833, and an Act of 1838 founded 'parliamentary schools' to plug holes in the existing system. A schools inspectorate was established in 1840 and in 1864 the government established a Royal Commission to investigate the system of education in Scotland, and to make recommendations. During the next three years it issued a series of reports, which led to the Education Act of 1872. The Act of 1872, which made schooling compulsory for all children from the age of five to fifteen, also brought the existing parish and burgh schools under the state control of a Scottish Education Department. The new drive for education created a rush of new school building projects and many new jobs for single women: the first professional opportunities for females.

The 1872 Act had shown that Scottish educationalist had never lost sight of in all the acts passed between the time of Knox and its preamble of which states that 'it is desirable to amend and extend the provisions of the law of Scotland on the subject of education, in such manner that the means of procuring efficient education for their children may be furnished and made available to the whole people of Scotland.' Writing in 1880, J Currie an early biographer of Robert Burns, could boast with considerable justification:

> A slight acquaintance with the peasantry of Scotland would service to convince an unprejudiced observer that they possess a degree of intelligence not generally found among the same class of men in the other countries of Europe. In the very humblest condition of the Scottish peasants every once can read, and most persons are more or less skilled in writing and arithmetic; and under the disguise of their uncouth appearance, and of the peculiar manners and dialect, a stranger will discover that they possess a curiosity, and have obtained a degree of information corresponding to these requirements.

Chapter Six

WORKING LIFE

By the beginning of the nineteenth century, Scotland was no longer simply a nation of rural workers and landowners, but increasingly a nation of town-dwellers and industrial workers. Glasgow, by 1801 Scotland's largest city, epitomised every aspect of this development with its smokestacks, brick factories, and glowing foundries jostling with streets and tenements where the workers huddled in appalling living conditions. Sir Walter Scott expressed the concerns of many when he wrote:

> The state of society now leads so much to great accumulations of humanity that we cannot wonder if it ferment and reek like a compost dunghill. Nature intended that population should be diffused over the soil in proportion to its extent. We have accumulated in huge cities and smothering manufactories the numbers which should be spread over the face of a country and what wonder that they should be corrupted? We have turned healthful and pleasant brooks into morasses and pestiferous lakes.

Before the eighteenth century industries in Scotland were run on a local basis and the numbers employed in them were still relatively small. The importance of the coal and salt industries was underlined by an act of parliament in 1606 that established the hereditary status of male and female serfs to work in those industries. The workers were the property of the owners and could not leave. It made their work largely hereditary and set such workers apart from the rest of the community. In compensation the master was obliged to keep his serfs all their days, in sickness and old age, and to supply a coffin for their burial. This extraordinary state of bondage did not end until 1775, when an Act was passed to emancipate all who after that date 'shall begin to work as colliers and salters', all those already working who were under twenty-one years of age, who were to be set free in seven years, and those between twenty-one and thirty who were to be liberated in ten years. It was not until 1799 that an Act finally freed Scottish colliers completely.

Coal was important because with wood in short supply it and peat were the only means of heating and cooking. Coal heughs, or outcrops, where coal is near the surface of the ground, were largely worked out by the end of the sixteenth century. New deep mines and coal shafts were now beginning to be opened. Salt, used as a vital food preservative, was used in such quantities that by 1590 it was the third most valuable import into Scotland after iron and timber. Salt-panning had long been practised on the east and west coasts of Scotland, but Lothian landowners like the Seton family were now developing the industry on a large scale.

At the beginning of the eighteenth century woollen manufacture was the leading domestic industry in Scotland. The woollen industry's origins were ancient, but it was not until the sixteenth century that the Scottish Parliament

Canonmills Loch. From James Grant, Old & New Edinburgh, *issued in weekly instalments c.1890.*

were taking active steps to promote it in response to the increasing popularity of English-made cloth which it was feared would ruin domestic manufacturers. An Act was accordingly passed in 1597, which denounced 'the hame-bringing of English claith, the same claith having only for the maist part an outward show, wanting that substance and strength whilk ofttimes it appears to have.' The Scottish Parliament was concerned that the importation of English cloth was the chief cause of 'transporting of all gold and silver furth of this realm, and consequently of the present dearth of the cuntyie.' Parliament forbade the exportation of wool, and, in 1705, enacted that all bodies being prepared for burial should be buried wrapped in woollen cloth.

Spinning was the occupation of most women, while weavers wrought the wool into plaidings, blankets and hodden gray. There were villages and towns where weavers produced goods of such quality that they became associated with the product – Glasgow plaidings, Aberdeen fingrams, Kilmarnocks, Musselburgh stuffs. By the nineteenth century the woollen industry was able to specialise successfully in higher quality production, notably in three branches: the manufacture of tweeds, hosiery and carpets. The growth of the Border tweed industry, centred especially on Galashields, was facilitated by the use of the power loom in the manufacture of narrow cloths, the increasing interest in the Lowlands of tartan patterns, and the availability of supplies of wool from Australia, New Zealand and South America.

By 1825, nearly 25,000 people were employed in the various branches of woollen manufacture in Scotland and by 1862, 82 mills used 1,069 power looms giving full-time employment to an increasing number of women. According to David Bremner, *The Industries in Scotland: Their Rise, Progress and Present Condition,* (1869):

The looms are superintended by young women, who earn large wages, and to whom the work is well suited, as it is easy and healthy. They have simply to look out for and mend broken threads, keep the shuttles supplied with yarn, and remove any knots or imperfections in the work. The handloom weavers had a strong prejudice against the power-looms, and would not relinquish their old-fashioned machines and go to work with the new; hence females were set to do the work. Ultimately the men came to think that they should overcome their prejudices, and many of them would fain take charge of the power-looms; but the women having got possession, determined to keep it, and minding a power-loom is now regarded as a woman's and a womanly occupation.

Linen had been a major industry in Scotland for hundreds of years. An Englishman touring the Highlands in 1618 stated that 'the houses of the gentry are like castles, and the master of the house's beaver is his blue bonnet; he will wear no shirts but of the flax that grows on his own ground, or of his wife's, daughters', or servants' spinning; his hose, stockings, and jerkins are made of his own sheep's wool.' Another visitor in 1725 noted 'Many of the Scotch ladies are good housewives, and many gentlemen of good estate are not ashamed to wear the clothes of their wives and servants' spinning.'

By 1795, nearly 39,000 handloom weavers were at work in Scotland. These linen workers were cottagers, working in their own homes and hand-made wheels and frames. These cottagers were busy making Holland sheeting and shirtings, linen for umbrellas and window blinds, the famous shawl cloths, calicoes and muslins, besides the stiff linens used mainly for hat linings. Individual towns had their famous products, such as the fine lawns and damasks of Glasgow, and the coarse linens and bleached canvas produced in Fife which were used by the Navy, the table linen from Dunfermline, and the renowned Paisley twisted thread. On every farm, minister's glebe and nearly every laird's house, a parcel of ground was devoted to growing flax and making yarn became an increasing occupation in every household and village. According to John Naismith, In the *Old Statistical Account* for Hamilton:

> the principal employment of the women in this parish has long been the spinning of linen yarn; packs of which were collected and sent to England, about the beginning of this century, besides what was made into cloth at home. So late as the year 1750, large parcels of yarn were sent from Hamilton to the north of Ireland: but the Irish have since learned to make good yarn, to supply their own demands; and the manufacture at home has consumed all the yarn, made in this neighbourhood. The state of manufacture has, of late, undergone considerable alterations. Formerly, almost all the weavers manufactured linen only, and either employed themselves,

or derived their employment from others on the spot. Now they get employment from the great manufacturers in Glasgow, &c. and cotton yarn is the principal material. Young women, who were formerly put to the spinning wheel, now learn to slower muslin, and apply to the agents of the same manufacture for employment.

Scots took considerable pride in their industry as Miss Mure of Caldwell recalled: 'I remember in the year 1730 or 1731 of a ball, when it was agreed that the company should be dressed in nothing but what was manufactured in the country; my sisters were as well dressed as any, and their gowns were stripped linen at 2s. 6d., with fourpenny edging from Hamilton, all the best that could be had'.

Weaving became mechanised from the 1820s and 1830s and hand-weaving disappeared during the late nineteenth century. New machines and greater power changed the textile industry in Scotland from a home industry to one based on the factory. It offered a very different working life to those employed in the linen trade. One such factory was that of Beveridge & Co as described by David Bremner in 1869:

In addition to the 900 power-looms in St Leonard's factory, Messrs Beveridge & Co. employ 180 hand-looms in a separate workshop. Altogether they give employment to about 1500 persons, of whom about ninety per cent. are females. The quantity of linen made by the firm averages about 200,000 square yards a-week, so that the yearly produce, supposing the average width of the web to be one yard, amounts to 10,400,000 yards, or upwards of 5900 miles, which would be sufficient to cover a board at which the entire population of Scotland and Ireland might dine at one time...The women and girls employed in the factory earn from 4s. to 15s. a-week, and the men from 10s. to 40s. Many of the women and a few of the man live at a considerable distance, and, when they go to work in the morning, take their day's provisions with them. Two large dining-halls are provided for their accommodation at meal time. These are comfortably fitted up, and adjoining them is a large stove for warming food.

By the 1780s, the cotton industry had become increasingly important. Cotton had formerly been only the preserve of the rich. 'Now', David

Old Broughton, 1825. From James Grant, Old & New Edinburgh, *issued in weekly instalments c.1890*

Macpherson wrote in 1786 in his *Annals of Commerce*, 'Now cotton is cheaper than linen yarn, and cotton goods are very much used in place of cambric. Women of all ranks, from the highest to the lowest, are clothed in British manufactures of cotton from the muslin cap on the crown of the head to cotton stockings under the sole of the feet. With gentlemen cotton stuffs for waistcoats have almost superseded woollen cloth and silk stuff'.

The cotton industry was based mainly in Lanarkshire and Renfrewshire; from the 1851 census, over 37,000 people in Glasgow were involved directly or indirectly in cotton manufacturing, out of a population of 360,000. The larger cotton mills established in the later eighteenth century were unlike anything that had gone before changing the landscape of many towns and villages across Scotland. Their size – New Lanark employed about 1,700 in 1820 – alone made them unique. Mills owners faced the considerably problem of finding an adequate labour supply, especially those established in more remote areas near a good water supply. The costs of construction of such mills meant that many remained in the initial location even when steam power was used in them. They met their labour supply by using pauper children and by encouraging migrants from rural Scotland and from Ireland. Henry Houldsworth, who had mills in Anderston and Woodside in Glasgow commented in 1833 that they were 'almost full of Irish; we can scarcely get a Scotchman for a partner or a watchman'. He was also very critical of some of the local labour which he had initially employed:

> At that period the spinning trade was extremely limited; there was not, I believe, more than one mill or so at Glasgow; at that time the hands employed were principally highland men, and all the attempts that were made to induce those men to work hard and live better were of no avail, and I had to get Englishmen to show them an example of industry before I could stir; for the first six months I could not get them to earn more than 12s. to 14s. a week; they would rather live upon meal and potatoes than exert themselves, but they were more sober than they are now.

These mills brought with them overcrowded and squalid conditions particularly in the smaller establishments. Squalor and harsh industrial discipline were found more often in the smaller concerns. According to a report of the Factories Inquiry Commissioners in 1833 at Stirling a number of woollen and paper factories 'are kept in a very fifthly state, ill ventilated, and the machinery is not well boxed'. At Blantyre the Commissioners found:

> The Blantyre works belonging to Messrs. Henry Monteith and Company is the only great establishment which I have seen, situated in the country, away from the population of a town, of which it is impossible to write chiefly in terms of approbation. The buildings are most of them old, the apartments are not well cleaned, low-roofed, the passages narrow, ventilation little attended to, there are no seats for the workers, and occasionally considerable annoyance from the water closets.

In some of the larger concerns – New Lanark, Catrine and Deanson – the proprietors took steps to improve, not only working conditions, but the environment in which their workers lived. Housing was provided which was a considerable improvement to that in the surrounding countryside. At the custom-built cotton-spinning village of New Lanark, begun in 1785 by

David Dale and taken to even greater heights by Dale's son-in-law Robert Owen who bought it from him in 1800, a series of social and educational reforms designed to improve the quality of life for his workforce were introduced. These included phasing out the use of child labour and establishing progressive schools, including the world's first nursery school. The village store at New Lanark, which under Owen was run for the benefit of the community, is now regarded as the cradle of the co-operative movement. Prices were kept low by bulk buying, and the profits helped to meet the running expenses of the schools. David Dale, in common with many of his contemporaries in the textile industry, entered into agreements with charity workhouses in Glasgow and Edinburgh to take on orphan or pauper children as apprentices. These children were given no wages, but were provided with food and clothing and a basic education. They were housed in the upper part of Mill Four, and although the apartments were basic, they were kept clean, and well aired.

The mechanisation of the textile industry did not lead to the immediate destruction of the handloom industry as it popularly supposed. Much of the output of yarn from the new spinning mills was woven in Scotland and so increased the demand for the services of the handloom weavers. Their number probably doubled from 1780 to something under 60,000 in 1800. From the 1780s to about 1815, while demand for their services was high, handloom weavers earned as much as 30s. a week which gave them considerable status above other workmen. The introduction of the power loom, used successfully at Catrine in 1807 and soon afterwards at other Finlay establishments, challenged their supremacy, but before 1820, when the power loom had still not been adopted extensively in cotton weaving, the numbers of handloom weavers actually increased to over 80,000 in 1840. The great Glasgow cotton merchant Kirkman Finlay summed the situation up in 1833: 'A great mistake exists in supposing that powerlooms supplant the handloom weaver ... the latter can make a great many things which it would not be in the interest of any powerloom manufacture to make, especially all the finest goods'.

The handloom weavers were generally located in a certain quarter of the Lowland towns, in areas still commemorated as Weavers' Row. By the 1860s, however, their numbers declined as, year by year earnings fell as local manufacturers slashed wages in order to cut prices in order to meeting the challenge of overseas competitors. This decline in wages was accelerated with the influx of migrants from the Highlands and in particular Ireland.

New Lanark. From a postcard. Author's collection

The report of Jellinger Symons, the Assistant Commissioner for the South of Scotland, to the Hand-loom Weavers Commission in 1839 summed up the situation:

> The Irish weavers are a little in advance in the career down hill, for they are the main cause of pulling the Scotch down after them. Of course they are in a slightly better condition than in their own country, which is precisely the reason why they take the lead in the career downwards, having less natural repugnance to privations which they have been previously in some measure inured to; when a manufacturer desires to lower wages, it is ten to one but the Irish are the first to accept his terms.

Many handloom weavers had therefore little option but to enter other occupations. Some entered the factories, others emigrated. Those who remained were faced with an uncertain future as David Bremner noted in 1869: 'In. busy times, the "rickle-tick" of the looms may be heard issuing from every door and window, and a stranger might have the impression that he was in the midst of a hive of industry in which the bees could not fail to have every comfort and happiness. But there are frequent gloomy, weary days, in which the shuttle lies at rest, and the men hang about the doors with sad countenances, or saunter to the factory to ascertain what prospect there is of obtaining another job.'

The modern iron industry was pioneered by Scotland by Carron Company when it was founded in 1759 to smelt with coke and use both the coal and ironstone. Carron was soon the largest foundry in Europe. The operations carried on within the works were long kept secret from the outside and visitors, including Robert Burns, were not encouraged. The poet, angered by being prevented from seeing the works, gave vent to his feelings by scratching the following lines on a pane of a window of a local inn at Carron:

We cam' na here to view your warks,
In hopes to be main wise,
But only, lest we gang to hell,
It may be na'e surprise;
But when we titled at your door,
Your porter dought na hear us;
Sae may, should we to hell's yetts come,
Your billy Satan sair us!

By 1869, although in decline, David Bremner was still impressed by the scale of great works at Carron:

On approaching the works by the long irregularly built street leading in an almost direct line from Grahamston, the visitor's eye is first attracted by the flames of five blast furnaces which stand on the south side of the works. The smaller flames issuing from the chimneys of the cupola and air-furnaces next arrest attention; and a nearer approach brings into view a whole forest of chimneys, shooting up from amid vast ranges of brick-built workshops. On getting inside the boundaries of the establishment the mere sightseer would probably be somewhat disappointed. The great extent of the place does not become apparent until the various departments are visited in succession; nor can it be said that externally the workshops present an inviting appearance. But within those ragged- looking and smoke-begrimed structures, processes go on which illustrate some of the grandest developments of human ingenuity; and in no individual establishment, in this country at least, can such a variety of operations in the manufacture of iron be seen. As one passes through the place, the roar of furnaces, the clash of machinery, and the clatter of anvils, fall upon the ear from all sides, and combined with the irregular nature of the roadways, the immense and apparently confused piles of iron, old and new, and of finished and unfinished articles of every conceivable form, produce a most bewildering effect on persons unaccustomed to such sounds and scenes.

The development of the iron industry went hand in hand with that of the coal-mining industry. Coal was required to fire the boilers which produced the steam which drove the engines and to heat the furnaces in which iron was smelted. Iron provided the frames, rollers, cylinders and pistons from which the new machinery was made. Coal-mining in the seventeenth and eighteenth centuries had been limited to part of Fife, Ayrshire and Lanarkshire and mainly to surface mining. With the increase in demand for coal in the eighteenth century a number of new pits were opened, and older seams extended. In the early nineteenth century the industry expanded, particularly in Ayrshire, Lanarkshire, the Lothians, and Fife, so that by the middle of that century the Scottish mines produced some seven and a half

Dundee Murraygate. Postcard. Author's collection

million tons a year, a considerable amount of which was exported. By 1900 this total had reached thirty-three million tons.

For all this success a heavy price was paid by the people whose labour made it all happen. Work in 'heavy' industries and in textile production was unhealthy and often dangerous for the men, women and children who worked long hours for miserably low wages. Even away from their work the workers could not escape from the consequences of industrialisation. Their homes, often built by the employers conveniently close to the place of employment, were all too commonly slums; over-crowded, insanitary and polluted by smoke and fumes from factories and railway yards. The harsh character of factory labour was reflected in many contemporary accounts. James Myles reflected on his first days at a Dundee mill around 1815:

> When I went to a spinning mill I was about seven years of age. I had to get out of bed every morning at five o'clock, commence work at half-past five, drop at nine for breakfast, begin again at half-past nine, work until two, which was the dinner hour, start again at half-past two, and continue until half-past seven at night. Such wee the nominal hours; but in reality there were no regular hours, masters and managers did with us as they liked. The clocks at the factories were often put forward in the morning and back at night, and instead of being instruments for the measurement of time, they were used as cloaks for cheatery and oppression.

The age at which children started work depended on the income of their parents and what occupation they hoped to follow. Even before the Industrial Revolution it was common for girls to help their mothers at spinning or winding flax or wool from the age of six or seven, and for boys to be sent out to work as herds for the farmer at the age of seven or eight. For many children, the first experience of work, by the later nineteenth century was a part-time job out of school hours. In Dundee before the First World War, some 5000 girls between the ages of twelve and fourteen, were working either as 'half-timers' or as whole-timers exempted from further attendance at school during the day after having passed the necessary standards, but not exempted from school altogether.

The half-timers either went to work and to the board school on alternative days, or went to special factory schools run by the largest employers like Buists or Baxters, where they were employed for half the day as 'shifters' in the mill and spent the other half in the classroom. Far worse off were the whole-timers, who from the age of thirteen worked in the mill for five days a week from 6am to 6pm and were then, by order of Dundee School Board, made to attend evening school from 7:15 to 9:15 until they were fourteen. The Certifying Factory Surgeon was extremely critical: 'It is a terrible strain – a long, long day for even a grown woman. If the girl is not very much above the average strength this is sure to tell very seriously. Is it to be wondered at, that they become languid, anemic and stunted, growing into womanhood with a decided appearance that Nature had intended them to be women of much greater physical strength'.

The Children's Employment Commission of 1840 was one of the most shocking documents of its time. Its inspectors, who had been sent out to investigate whether the provisions of a series of factory acts limiting the working hours of apprentices and children were being implement, decided also to examine conditions in the mines. In mining towns baby girls were disparagingly described as 'a hutch of dross' while boys were 'a hutch of coal'. Even so, girls and women were enormously useful in the mines, partly because they could make themselves helpful at a younger age, and this start work earlier, and partly because of their willingness to crawl into the most uncomfortable areas without complaint.

The Commission's report so horrified the public that a law was passed making it illegal for women and children to go down the pits. This legislation heightened the misery for those women for whom the pit was their only source of income. To evade the law, some disguised themselves as men; their co-workers turned a blind eye. The foreman at Ormiston colliery told the commission:

> In fact women always did the lifting or heavy part of the work and neither they nor the children were treated like human beings where they are employed. Females submit to work in places where no man or even lad could be got to labour in; they work in bad roads, up to their knees in water, their posture almost double. They are below till the last hour of pregnancy. They have swelled ankles and haunches and are prematurely brought to the grave or, what is worse, to a lingering existence.

Janet Cumming, coal bearer aged eleven, told the Commissioners:

I gang with the women at five and come up at five at night; work all night on Fridays and come away at twelve in the day. The roof is very low; I have to bend my back and legs and the water is frequently up to the calves of my legs. Have no liking for the work. Father makes me like it.

Often whole families worked down the pit. Those who dug the coal (hewers) were paid by the amount of coal carried to the surface. Hewers therefore often paid their wives and children to carry the coal. These workers, coal bearers and putters, worked extremely hard for long periods of time. Things had improved little by the end of the nineteenth century. American writer Kellogg Durland spent several months in the Fife mining community of Kelty in 1900:

The man with whom I was to work appeared, and I followed toward the ever increasing heat for nearly two hundred yards where the men were working naked to the waist, their streaming bodies streaked and begrimed with coal dust which permeated all the atmosphere till they seemed little like men. Breathing was an effort in spite of the current of air that passed through the passage. The monotonous click of the picks against the resisting coal fell on the ear like sounds from an unreal world, while from a distance the men who crouched or knelt before the grim wall, which they attacked with the brutal force of automatons, looked liked creaters damned for their sins, the muttered 'T-s-s-t – t-s-st, sish-s-sish, t-s-s-t' coming from between their half closed teeth with machine-like regularity.

Conditions were little better for the rapidly growing number of women who were employed in the industry. A letter from the principle agent of the Hamilton Estates to the Duchess, 1851: 'While the males were employed digging in the pits with pickaxes and shovels, the women were engaged in carrying the coal on their backs from the extremity of the mines, to the pit bottoms or mouths of the mines, or in dragging that mineral there by means of hutches or hurleys along the underground roads. Muscular strength in a female, not beauty, was the grand qualification by which she was estimated, and a strong young woman was sure of finding a husband readily. There is an old Scotch saying, 'She is like the collier's daughter, better than she is

Steam boat on the Clyde near Dumbarton. From William Daniell, Voyage Round Great Britain, *1820.*

bonny'.

The development of the railways brought about a second Industrial Revolution in Scotland. Edinburgh and Glasgow were linked by rail by 1842, and spur lines ran from the cities to the smaller towns in their areas. Railway connections with the south were established with the foundation in 1845 of the Caledonian Railway which linked Glasgow with the North Western Railway at Carlisle, and then to London. The social consequences were spectacular. The railway network integrated the country as never before, as travel was now possible for people with little leisure and no private transport. For the fortunate, railways made it possible to live at a distance from the place of employment, and suburbs arose around the cities, providing more work for architects, masons, builders, carpenters and slaters, plumbers and painters. Industrial costs were dramatically lowered and profits accordingly soared. Production of coal and iron (and steel) was greatly increased demand and new jobs at all levels were provided – labourers to lay the tracks and civil engineers to plan them; mechanical engineers to design locomotives; labourers to smelt the iron-ore; platers and riveters to build them; drivers and firemen to crew the engines, and signalmen and surfacemen to see to the safe scheduled running of the trains.

By the second half of the nineteenth century the iron industry with its attendants, coal-mining and engineering challenged the predominance of textiles in Scotland. In the final decades of that century ship-building and steel manufacture took the place of the iron industry. The central belt of Scotland had by that time become the most intensively industrialized regions in the world. By 1913, Glasgow, claiming for herself the title of 'Second City of the Empire', made, with her satellite towns, one-fifth of the steel, one-third of the railway locomotives and rolling stock, one-third of the shipping tonnage and one –half of the marine-engine horsepower in the United Kingdom.

The development of the heavy industries brought about an enormous change in the landscape of many parts of Scotland. With the spread of coalming and ironworking came the bings, the pit-shafts with their desolate buildings and coke-ovens, the criss-cross of mineral railways. In some parishes, notably the Monklands, existing hamlets grew rapidly and towns, such as Coatbridge, appeared from nothing. Those parts of the towns which had once been occupied by weavers were not interspersed by Victorian tenements while Irish and Highland immigration frequently brought in a rapid increase in Chapels. In such areas, especially in parts of north Lanarkshire and north Ayrshire, the harshness of life was evident. To Thomas Tancred, visiting Monklands parishes in 1842, it seemed that:

> Everything that meets the eye or ear tells of slavish labour united to brutal intemperance. At night, ascending to the hill on which the Established Church stands, the groups of blast-furnaces on all sides might be imagined to be blazing volcanoes, at most of which the smelting is continued Sundays and week-days, by day and night, without intermission. By day a perpetual steam arises from the whole length of the canal where it receives the waste-water from blast-engines on both sides of it; and railroads, traversed by long trains of wagons drawn by locomotive engines, intersect the country in all directions, and are the cause of frequent accidents, into which, by the law of Scotland, no inquiry is made.

Chapter Seven

RELIGION

The chief characteristic of the Scots that made the biggest impression on many travellers from south of the border was, in the words of John Macky in 1723, 'their religious soberness and decorous observance of the Sabbath'. He noted that 'there is nothing of the gaiety of the English, but a sedate gravity on every face, without the stiffness of the Spaniards; and I take this to be owing to their praying and frequent long graces which gives their looks a religious cast.' The Scots were denounced as a 'priest ridden people' but the Covenanting days had fostered in the population a love for the fiery preacher and a determination that they, and not their betters, would chose their minister.

The Scottish Reformation was the achievement of John Know, a preacher of truly legendary power. The church he established swept aside Scottish Catholicism which five century's earlier had been declared 'a special daughter' of the Roman see, subject only to the Pope. All manifestations of the old church were obliterated: monasteries and bishops, clerical vestments, holy relics and market-square crosses. Stained-glass windows were smashed, saints' statures, ripped out choir stalls and roodscreens and alters overturned. St Giles, Edinburgh, became the political as well as the religious heart of Scotland but according to early seventeenth century English traveller and writer Fynes Morrison it was without beauty or ornament:

> In this church the King's seat is built some few stairs high of wood, and leaning upon the pillar next to the pulpit, and opposite to the same is another seat very like it, in which the incontinent use to stand and do penance; and some few weeks past, a Gentleman,

John Knox by Hondius, after the Beze. British Museum

being a stranger and taking it for a place where men of better quality used to sit, boldly entered the same in sermon time, till he was driven away with the profuse laughter of the common sort, to the disturbance of the whole congregation.

Knox and his followers imposed the new rules of the Calvinist Sabbath on their contemporaries and many generations yet to come. The Reformation Sabbath began at six o'clock in the evening of Saturday and lasted for twenty-four hours. During this time there was to be no work done, no unseemly activities, no dancing, no playing of the pipes, no markets or frequenting of alehouses. Kirk-sessions arraigned women for selling candles and bread on the Sabbath, a miller for grinding corn and a poultry man for plucking geese.

Outside the Sabbath, action was taken by the Church against a whole range of offences. In 1578 the Kirk session of Perth ordered John Todd to stand in irons for two hours to expiate a slanderous speech. Other slanderers in Dumfries were ordered to 'stand at the kirk-stile on the Sabbath, with branks upon their mouths'. The brank was a padlocked helmet of iron, thrusting a triangular tongue into the victims mouth. When the minister of Jedburgh, Paul Methven admitted to adultery, he escaped execution, but was ordered to stand in sackcloth before his church, to sit on a pentitent's stool within.

Harsh and autocratic though this may seem, the form of Presbyterianism that developed in Scotland followed Knox's vision of political power, ordained by God, and vested not in kings or nobles or even the clergy, but in the people. George Buchannan, tutor to the infant James VI, carried these views even further. 'The people', he declared, have the right to confer the royal authority upon whomever they wish'. If the ruler failed to act in accordance with the law laid down by the people 'the lowest and meanest of men' had the right to resist. The minister was chosen by the congregation's consistory of elected elders, instead of by some aristocrat or laird. The elders also sent deputations to their local synod, who in turn sent representatives of the Kirk's General Assembly. It was the single most democratic system of church government in Europe and James VI, and his sons, showed their determination to reassert the power of the monarchy.

Though a convinced Protestant, James VI was no Presbyterian. He was strongly attached to the idea of episcopacy. 'No Bishop', he would say, 'no King'. In 1584 James induced the Scottish Parliament to pass statutes confirming the appointment of bishops and forbidding Convocations of ministers unless sanctioned by the King. These measures created a storm of opposition and in the end James was forced to give way. After he became King of England in 1603, James prevented the General Assembly from meeting until 1618 when he forced it to push through his Five Articles.

These stated that Holy Communion should be received kneeling; that the festivals of the Christian year should be observed; that confirmation should be administered by bishops and not by ministers; that private baptism and private Communion should be allowed in cases of series illness. They met with widespread opposition and were boycotted throughout much of Scotland.

Charles I learned nothing from his father's failures and took it upon himself to try to break the power and authority of the Presbyterian Church in Scotland. He unleashed a series of events which would not only cost him his crown but also his head. On 23 July 1637, when the dean of St Giles's in Edinburgh opened his Sunday morning service with the new Anglican Book of Common Prayer, as the King had ordered, he was greeted with shouts and insults from the women in the congregation; others threw stools while many more stormed out of the church. The riots which followed forced the Bishop of Edinburgh to flee for his life. In February 1638, ministers, nobles and ordinary citizens gathered in Greyfriars Church to sign a National Covenant. It challenged the King's prerogative to make law without consent, and affirmed that the Scottish people would oppose any change not approved by a free General Assembly and Parliament. Bands of signatories carried copies from Edinburgh to neighbouring towns and then the rest of the country.

In November the General Assembly in Glasgow declared war on 'the Kingdom of Satan and Antichrist', meaning Charles and his bishops. Thousands of volunteers flocked into the Covenanters' army, many armed only with hoes and scythes. They still managed to defeat Charles's invading mercenary army and forced the king to sue for peace. The Bishops' War as it became known encouraged Charles' opponents in the English Parliament leading to Civil War. Later, in 1647, when the King had lost his fight with Parliament, he offered the Scots religious freedom and state support of their Kirk if they would let him regain his Crown. Amazingly they agreed only to be defeated at the Battle of Preston by Oliver Cromwell.

On his return from exile in May 1660, Charles II showed that he was as determined as his father to bend the Scottish church to his will by imposing an Episcopalian establishment on Scotland. Covenanting ministers who opposed him were deprived of their parishes. But many parishioners remained loyal to them, especially in the south-west, and instead attended unauthorized and outlawed gatherings, known as conventicles, either in private houses or outdoors. The campaign against them was led by his

Secretary for Scotland, the Duke of Lauderdale, who ruled Scotland with an iron fist until 1680. These are remembered in Scottish history as 'the Killing Time'. Launderdale used military occupation, torture, execution and penal servitude in the West Indies to crush his opponents. His army was drawn from the pro-Stuart Highland clans, dubbed the Highland Host, which he led into the Covenanting southwest Lowlands.

The accession of the Charles' brother James caused even more consternation and his downfall three years later in 1688 was greeted in Scotland with considerable relief. Under William of Orange and Mary the Kirk regained its independence. The oath taken by William and Mary at their coronation, committed them to maintaining the 'true religion … now received and preached within the realm of Scotland'. Presbyterianism was re-established in June 1690 and the Kirk was given the right to purge 'all inefficient, negligent scandalous and erroneous ministers'. Two Commissions were set up, for the areas to the north and the south of the Tay to set the

St Giles, interior. From James Grant, Old & New Edinburgh, *issued in weekly instalments c.1890*

subsequent purge in motion. Over the next twenty-five years it would claim almost two-thirds of the ministry as its victims. Many presbyteries were left with few or no parish ministers but the church retained its dominant position as both the voice and the conscience of the people.

In Edinburgh, 'seizers' patrolled the streets during sermon-time to ensure attendance in the churches. Sir Richard Steele, founder of *The Tatler*, who visited Edinburgh in 1717, nicknamed the Reverend Andrew Hart 'the hangman of the Gospel' because he seemed to take such pleasure in preaching 'the *terrors* of the Lord'. In 1775 Captain Edward Topham, an English traveller, said that during Sunday service it was as if 'some epidemic disorder had depopulated the whole City'. Weekdays were only a little less sombre. Kirk elders went into the taverns at 10 p.m. by the church clock to send the occupants home. Visiting touring theatrical companies faced the wrath of the Kirk-sessions. As the Reverend George Anderson told the congregation at Edinburgh's Tron Church: 'A Life spent in innocent Diversions is in itself sinful ... By doing no Good you do evil'. An Act of the Edinburgh Presbytery of 29 April 1719 complained that:

> A great number take an unaccountable liberty in despising and profaning the [Lord's day] idly and wickedly, by standing in companies in the streets, misspending their time in idle discourse, vain and useless communications ... withdrawing from the city ... to take their recreations in walking the fields, parks, links, meadows ... And by entering into taverns, ale-houses, milk-houses, gardens, or other places, to drink, tipple, or otherwise misspend any part thereof; by giving or receiving civil visits ... and by idly gazing out of windows ...

By the middle of the eighteenth century Presbyterianism was in a comfortable ascendancy, although its strength varied greatly from region to region. The centre of its power lay in the central and southern Lowlands which had been the focus of the covenanting struggles of the seventeenth century. The Kirk session was the local court for all manner of minor civil as well as religious offences (ranging from Sabbath desecration and fornication to assault, wife-beating and infanticide). It was the collector and distributor of poor relief and issued 'testimonials' to allow migrants to be received in other parishes. The parish school was designed to educate all children, and the kirkyard was usually the only place for burials.

Those who were not members of the Kirk could find live difficult as George Fox, the founder of Quakerism, found when he visited Edinburgh in 1657:

> ...there friends had been in great sufferings for the Presbyterian priests had excommunicated them and that none might buy or sell with them nor eat nor drink with them, so they could neither sell their commodities nor buy what they wanted: so as it went very hard with some of them for if they had brought bread or victuals of any of their neighbours, the priest threatened them so with curses that they would run and fetch it from them again.

Quakerism was just one of the dangerous religious thinking coming up from the south. In 1695 the General Assembly of the Reformed Church recommended that ministers apply directly to civil magistrates for punishing cases of blasphemy and profanity. In 1696 a nineteen year old theology student Thomas Aikenhead shivering from the cold had declared as he passed the Tron Church in Edinburgh, 'I wish right now I were in the place Ezra called hell, to warm myself there'. One of his fellow students reported him to the Kirk authorities. When the Lord Advocate heard of this, and other remarks in which Aikenhead had said that Jesus Christ Himself was an impostor, he decided that these remarks constituted blasphemy as defined by the act of 1695, which decreed that a person 'not distracted in his wits', was to be punished by death. Aikenhead was executed on 8 January 1697.

Despite the dominance of the Presbyterian Church, by the early eighteenth century many churches were dark, very narrow buildings, with a few little windows having small panes of glass. The floors were earthen, and in some older kirks of the North, according to the *Scots Magazine* in 1886, 'the bodies of many generations had been buried beneath them, to the detriment of health, decency, and comfort; for sometimes the bones of the dead so strewed the floor that they were kicked by worshippers, who noses were afflicted by the "corrupt unripe corps" disturbed to make room for new tenants'. The *Statistical Accounts* of parishes written at the end of the eighteenth century contain many complaints from ministers of the deplorable condition of the places of worship at the time. One after another reports that the 'kirk is ruinous'; 'unhealthy, dark, cold, sunk beneath the surrounding earth'; and 'execrably filthy and out of repair'.

In a great many cases the buildings were so small as to give accommodation only to a third of the parishioners. The words of the minister of Glenorchy in 1792 expressed the feelings of many of his suffering congregation: 'With us, in the Church of Scotland, many of our country kirks are such dark, damp, dirty hovels as to chill and repulse every sentiment of devotion; they besides endanger the health of every class of worshippers, and encourage the indolent and indifferent in their negligence of instruction'. Thomas Pennant in his *Tour of Scotland*, published in the 1770s, found the thatched churches in such a woeful plight that he caustically observes, 'the people appear like the Druids to worship in an open temple'. He went on to declared that 'in many parts of Scotland our Lord seems still to be worshipped in a stable – and a very wretched one'.

It was well into the eighteenth century before most of the kirks were seated with fixed pews. Before that period the people stood during service, or sat on the stools or 'creepies' which they either brought with them each Sunday, or set aside in the church. According to the Kirk-Session records when disputes arose over their ownership or their occupancy they became

Rev Dr Walter Buchanan. From John Kay, A Series of Original Portraits, With Biographical Sketches and Illustrative Anecdotes. Edinburgh: A C Black, 1877

handy and formidable weapons and missiles. Gradually the custom became general for fixed pews to be set up. Parishioners of higher social position got permission from the Session to 'set up a desk' or seat for their family in a vacant space, and they removed it when they left the parish. At other times the Kirk-Sessions or magistrates put in forms or seats, which were let out to members of the congregation.

With the Act of Union in 1707, mass migration to the rapidly growing industrial towns, changes to the agricultural way of life, and dangerous new ideas from south of the border all contributed to changes in the religious outlook of many educated Scots. Commentators, such as the very pious Patrick Walker, noted the used of 'minced oaths; 'Not only,' it was noted, 'did Sabbath breaking abound to the extent that many before and after service walked in the fields', but 'even the professors, who never dreamed before of swearing, now dared to use such as expressions as "devil", "faith", "shame" and many have changed the blessed name of God into 'Gad' – one of his sinful mortal creatures'. In the olden days Walker comments 'they had golden ministers and wooden cups, now they have golden cups and wooden ministers'.

Despite the dominate position enjoyed by the Kirk, the eighteenth century saw increasingly polarisation of Scottish society. Two pieces of legislation passed in 1712 proved to be particularly controversial. The first granted religious toleration to the Episcopalians. The other removed the system instituted after 1690 under which ministers were appointed by all the heritors and elders of a parish and restored an earlier system whereby they were nominated by a single patron, generally a substantial landowner. This led to problems when, after 1730, patrons tried to install ministers who were not approved of by the bulk of their congregations. The clergy selected by patrons were invariably adherents of the 'Moderate' party which dominated the General Assembly of the Established Church from the 1750s until 1833.

By the 1740s a group of young ministers was increasingly troubled by the rising tide of disputes within the church and the challenge local congregations and their ministers were making to the authority of the General Assembly. In May 1751 a number of them, including Hugh Blair, Alexander Carlyle, John Home and William Robertson, met in an Edinburgh tavern to form the Moderate Party within the Kirk. The Moderates emphasised the need for order and subordination to authority within the Kirk. The involvement of many of the Moderates in philosophy and literature demonstrated their determination to make the church more liberal and secular in outlook and they opposed the traditional Calvinistic outlook of the evangelical wing of the church.

Moderates rejected the harsh Calvinist heritage of severe church discipline, fiery didactic sermons and proscription of pursuits like dancing, drinking and gambling. But in the country as a whole, Evangelicals were numerically dominant and controlled the local courts (presbyteries and synods) of the Church.

The General Assembly was obliged after 1729 to appoint 'riding committees' to travel to parishes and induct unpopular presentees on their congregations. It was said that when the philosopher John Reid was presented in 1737 by King's College, Aberdeen, to the living of New Machar – a country parish some ten miles from the town – he was set upon by men dressed in women's clothes and ducked in a pond; on the Sunday he first preached, relations stood on the pulpit stair with a drawn sword. The people (and notably women) obstructed the induction of unwelcome ministers, barring entry to the church, leading to violent scenes on many occasions with cavalry being called in by a patron to lead the new minister into his pulpit. In the Highlands the disputed settlement of a parish minister often occurred at the same time as a product of landowners' clearance of the peasantry in preparing estates for sheep farming. During evictions in Assynt in Sutherland in 1813, a minister newly selected by the patron was driven out by the people, resulting in the summoning of a navy cutter and a detachment of militia.

During the early eighteenth century landowners also began to distance themselves from the rest of the congregation by constructing 'lairds' lofts' for themselves and their families. Proprietors increasingly claimed the right to annex a percentage of the floorspace in their local churches equivalent to the proportion of land they held in the parish. They then erected their own pews and allocated the seats in them. In the towns the system of pew-renting, which had existed in most burgh churches since the mid-seventeenth century, had traditionally been used to provide all social groups with access to community worship. Glasgow Town Council, for example, which owned and managed nearly all the Established churches in the city up to the 1810s, had until the 1780s allocated free church seats to the very poor, reserved large numbers of 'low-rented' seats (under 2/6d per annum) for the 'lower classes of inhabitants', and set aside pews for the inmates of city pauper institutions. At the other end of the social scale, seats were allocated to university staff, students, the town council and members of the incorporated trades; some seats were owned by wealthy families, and some seats were rented to individuals by virtue of long-standing family tradition. Only after all these seats were distributed were the remainder rented out, often by 'roup' (auction).

This system of ensuring widespread access to urban parish churches broke down in most burghs around 1800. In Glasgow between 1782 and 1812, there were large and repeated rent increases as demand rose with population increase, and low-rented and gratis seats were removed or made available for renting to the highest bidder. The system spread across all denominations (with the partial exception of the Baptists) and to every part of the country in the late eighteenth century. This was the cause of much of the non-churchgoing by unskilled and lower-paid workers. The need to pay seat rents six-monthly in advance exacerbated the financial difficulties of casual and seasonal workers. The Glasgow City Mission, in its first annual report of 1827, noted that a quarter of all the seats in the city's churches were empty, and identified the main cause as the high level of pew rents. But it also noted the need for fine clothes to attend church.

St Giles, 1853. London & Edinburgh: A Fullarton & Co, 1853.

The result was a return to the kind of field preaching last seen in the persecution years of the later Stuarts. Beginning in 1741, the English evangelist Methodist preacher George Whitefield made numerous visits to Edinburgh where he addressed crowds said to be over fifteen thousand strong in St Giles Churchyard, the Canongate Church, the King's Park and the grounds of Trinity Hospital. The revival reached its climax at the famous 'Cambuslang Wark' in Lanark the following year. Led by William McCulloch, minister of Cambuslang, who was in the habit of preaching out of doors, in the nearly gorge, because of the poor repair of the church. This lasted for about seven or eight months, until the coming of autumn. The event reached a great climax on 15 August 1742, when a crowd of some 30,000 gathered from all over the Lowlands in the 'preaching braes' – a natural amphitheatre next to the Kirk 'bathed in tears'. 'Such a Passover has not been heard of', Whitefield wrote. According to the *OldStatistical Account*:

> The way in which the converts were affected, for it seems they were all affected much in the same way, though in very different degrees, is thus described. They were seized all at once, commonly by something said in the sermons or prayers, with the most dreadful apprehensions concerning the state of their souls, insomuch that many of them could not abstain from crying out in the most public and dreadful manner, ... The agony under which they laboured, was expressed not only by words, but also by violent agitations of body; by clapping their hands and beating their breasts; by shaking and trembling; by faintings and convulsions; and sometimes by excessive bleeding at the nose. While they were in this distress, the minister often called out to them, not to stifle or smother their convictions, but to encourage them; and, after sermon was ended, he retired with them to the manse, and frequently spent the best part of the night with them in exhortations and prayers.

As many found themselves excluded from the local congregation by charging high pew rents, other agencies attempted to fill the gap. The first agency was the Sunday school, popularised by Robert Raikes of Gloucester in the 1780s. By keeping child workers from running loose on the streets and fields on the Sabbath and preventing them form burglarising worshippers' homes whilst attending church, the Sunday school attracted considerable attention from urban evangelicals. Initially using paid teachers, town councils sanctioned the establishment of 'Sabbath exercises' in Edinburgh, Aberdeen and Glasgow in the 1780s. The Sabbath School Union for Scotland claimed by 1819 the affiliation of 567 schools with 38,000 children attending.

After years of growing discontent with the Moderates, over a third of the clergy of the Church of Scotland signed a Deed of Demission in 1843, left their manses and formed their own church, the Free Church of Scotland under the leadership of Thomas Chalmers. This is an event rememberd as 'The Great Disruption'. Seceding ministers were turning their backs on a secure income and were now dependent on the financial support of their new congregation. One adherent to the new church, Argyllshire minister Reverend McLean recalled that he received a call from the local landowner 'the proprietor of more than one-half of the parish' who pressed him to remain with the church congratulating him on its being 'a model parish, educationally, a as well as otherwise, under my auspices, and he had hoped for himself and his children long to enjoy the blessing of my ministry'. Finding that he could not dissuade the Reverenced McLean 'from that day forth he exerted himself to the very utmost when we became houseless to keep us so, and have us exterminated altogether as a nuisance from the district.' On the Sunday that he was to leave the church he preached to his flock on the green in front of the manse:

> ... special care was taken to produce the impression among the people that, if I ventured to preach, measures were all ready and constables at hand for my forcible removal ... Entirely disregarding the threats, I felt it to be my duty to take my stand there; and there, accordingly, in the presence of my presecutors, who kept waling around about us, speaking loudly within earshot, and with significant looks, I conducted public worship, with such emotions as I may never feel again; while my poor flock, apprehensive every moment of what might happen, sat closer and closer together, like a fluttered covey when the hawk sails overhead ...

The Disruption led to a decline in the authority of the Church of Scotland. In Aberdeen every minister had gone over to the Free Church: over much of the Highlands defection to the Free Church was almost complete. In Glasgow and Edinburgh the division was more equally balanced, and in the Borders the Church of Scotland retained the loyalty of its members. The Free

Church had to build its own churches and schools and finance its own minister entirely from voluntary contributions. In 1851 the religious census taken by the Government indicated that the numbers attending the Church of Scotland and the Free Church were almost the same.

By the nineteenth century, the Roman Catholic Church was also gaining ground for the first time since the Reformation. The Jacobite risings in 1715 and 1745 had damaged the Catholic cause in Scotland and it was not until the start of Catholic Emancipation in 1793 that Roman Catholicism regained a civil respectability. During the nineteenth century, Irish immigration substantially boosted the number of Scottish Roman Catholics, especially in the west, and by 1900 it was estimated that 90–95% of Scottish Catholics were fully or partly of Irish descent.

In the Highlands, there had always been great resistance to Presbyterianism. This was reinforced in the seventeenth century when priests from Ireland came to the islands and Western Highlands as missionaries and established a strong Roman Catholic community which survives in certain areas to the present day. The movement of first Highland and then Irish Catholics to the west-central Lowlands in search of industrial

Tron Church. From Views in Edinburgh and its Vicinity: Drawn and Engraved by J and H S Storer. 1820, London

employment created severe logistical problems for a Church which, to all intents and purposes, did not exist in the region. In the 1770s, priests travelled from Perth and Edinburgh to minister to the twenty or so Catholics in Glasgow, and in the 1790s priests migrated with their Highland flocks to the city and its environs. By the 1830s Catholics made up about 13 per cent of Glasgow's population with higher concentrations developing in nearby industrial districts like Old Kirkpatrick, Renfrewshire and Monklands.

The re-emergence of the Roman Catholic Church in Scotland was one of the contributing factors that saw a revival of religious zeal and a sterner theological tone more in keeping with the outlook of Victorian Scotland. The Victorian Sabbath was a solemn occasion. A universal stillness fell over Glasgow and Edinburgh at the time of divine service, and pervaded small towns and villages from dawn to dusk. The son of a small businessman born in 1865 recalled:

> Sunday at home was a dismal ordeal for the younger generation. All newspapers and books of a secular character were carefully put out of sight. After breakfast, preparations were made for the Church. Black clothes were taken from the wardrobe and carefully brushed, clean linen was taken from the chest of drawers, boots were polished, and when everything was ready the whole family was marched to Church for the eleven o'clock service.

The Scots remained a church-going nation throughout the nineteenth century. In the middle of the century, the popular Edinburgh cleric the Dean Edward Ramsay records experiences of travellers on the Sabbath. A geologist was breaking some specimen minerals with a pocket hammer when he was approached by an old man on his way to church who said quietly, 'Sir, ye're breaking something there forbye the stanes!' An English artist asked a local man the name of a picturesque castle he was passing. The reply was 'It's no the day to be speerin' sic things!'

Chapter Eight

THE MILITARY

Scottish soldiers constituted one of the country's most successful export industries from the Middle Ages. As early as the late ninth century, Charles III of France was reputed to have had a Scottish bodyguard and in the mid-thirteenth century a Scottish force fought in the Eight Crusade under Louis IX. After the founding of the Auld Alliance with France in 1295, many Scots served with the French forces during the fourteenth and fifteenth centuries and by the early seventeenth century some 10,000 Scots were serving under Gustavus Adolphus in Sweden. Although it had been recruiting Lowland Regiments for two centuries, it was not until the middle of the eighteenth century that the British government took the controversial step of raising Highland regiments, recruited from clansmen who only a few years early had fought for Prince Charlie at Culloden. For the next two centuries the Highlander would prove their loyalty in countless Imperial wars.

Major Scottish armies from the early Middle Ages to the sixteenth century were based on a general call-out of able-bodied males between the ages of sixteen and sixty who were liable to serve in the defence of the kingdom at a time of crisis, at their own expense, for a period of forty days. This army was mobilized and led on a provincial basis (especially north of the Forth) by territorial earls, such as the lords of Carrick, Strathearn, or Lennox, while royal sheriffs and burgh officers were responsible for the turnout of eligible males in their own jurisdictions. In times of national emergency or rebellion individual kings did have recourse to paid troops and there were certain fulltime professionals, such as crossbowmen and, latterly, artillery gunners, who skills could not be maintained in the general levy and who were therefore paid by the crown.

This Scottish host was overwhelmingly an army of infantrymen composed of masses of ordinary peasants, merchants and townsmen, typically with little in the way of body armour except for an iron headpiece, padded jacket and gloves. The distinctive infantry weapon was the longshafted speak or pike, supplemented in some cases by a sword. In the medieval period, despite numerous Acts of Parliament encouraging archery practice, Scotland did not devote the time, effort and money to training and building a powerful force of archers. The only useful force of archers which Scotland could raise came from the hunters and woodsmen who lived in the Forest of Ettrick, in the borders.

The Union of the Crowns in 1603 brought to an end the need to raise a Scottish army to deal with an English invasion. Instead, under the Stuart Kings, armies were raised to enforce Royal policies and suppress opposition. During the First Civil War, 1642 to 1645, the Margquis of Montrose, as Charles I's Lieutenant, raised an army in Scotland composed partly of Irish mercenaries and partly of Highlanders. He fought a series of brilliant battles in a campaign lasting a year before his army was surprised by a superior force under General Leslie and routed at the battle of Philphaugh. When Charles II was declared King in Scotland, Leslie raised some 22,000 troops which successfully thwarted Cromwell for a time before being routed at Dunbar. About 10,000 prisoners were taken and a number of these finally sold as bond-servants in the colonies.

Captain James Burnet. From John Kay, A Series of Original Portraits, With Biographical Sketches and illustrative Anecdotes. Edinburgh: A C Black, 1877

The notorious Highland Host of 1678, consisting of 5,000 Highlanders and 3,000 regular troops, was used by Charles II as a device for suppressing the operation of conventicles in the south-west as a source of tensions between the second generation of Covenanters and the Scottish state. This period also saw the formation of the first Lowland Regiments the Royal Scots and the Royal Scots Fusiliers. The Royal Scots (The Royal Regiment), once known as the Royal Regiment of Foot, was the oldest, and therefore most senior, infantry regiment of the line in the British Army, having been originally raised in 1633 during the reign of Charles I of Scotland. The Royal Scots had been originally raised by Sir John Hepburn for service under Gustavus Adolphus. A second was subsequently raised largely from Scots in

Military Promenade. From John Kay, A Series of Original Portraits, With Biographical Sketches and Illustrative Anecdotes. Edinburgh: A C Black, 1877

France in 1633. Because the regiment had been formed by Royal Warrant, it was legally part of the Crown's armed forces, even though it had been out of the country for three decades. As such, it was recalled to help secure the coronation of Charles II, and helped provide a model for the other regiments founded after the collapse of the New Model Army.

The Royal Scots Fusiliers was raised in Scotland in 1678 by Stuart loyalist Charles Erskine, 5th Earl of Mar, for service against the rebel covenanting force. In the Glorious Revolution of 1689, the regiment was ordered south. Initially they stayed loyal to James II of England until he fled to Ireland, upon which they opted to serve Prince William of Orange. The regiment later ironically fought against the Jacobites during the 1745 Jacobite Rebellion at the Battle of Culloden. For more than four hundred years more Lowlanders than Highlanders would serve in the British army, but Scotland would become so associated with the Highland regiments that Lowland ones like the Royal Scots and the King's Own Scottish Borderers would later wear tartan trews as their ceremonial, or dress, uniform.

Other than suppressing political opposition, from 1642 the Crown also raised Independent Companies consisting solely of Highlanders to form a police-force to maintain law and order in the Highlands. In August 1667, Charles II issued a commission to the Earl of Atholl to raise and keep such a number of men as he should think fit 'to be a constant guard for ensuring the peace of the Highlands' and 'to watch upon the braes' his jurisdiction to extend to 'the shyres of Inverness, Nairn, Murray, Banff, Aberdeen, Mairnes, Angus, Perth, Clackmannan, Monteith, Stirling and Dumbarton'.

After the 1715 Jacobite Rising, clans loyal to the Stuarts raised a levy of troops to prowl the glens to suppress the remaining rebels. Although a Disarming Act was passed forbidding the carrying of arms in the Highlands, little was done to enforce it. It was not until 1725 and afterwards, when the Irish General George Wade set about building his military roads through the Highlands, that anything effective could be done to enforce such Acts. Wade raised six Independent Companies each consisting of 500 men, recruited with the intention of preventing theft and disorder and of enforcing the Disarming acts. The majority of the Highlanders recruited for these forces were the Presbyterian and Whig clans of Campbell, Grant and Fraser. General Wade issued a dark-blue-and-green tartan for these companies of Highlanders earning them the nickname *am Freicaeden Dubh* (Black Watch) in contrast to *Saighdearan Dearg* (Red Soldiers), the regulars in their scarlet tunics.

In 1734 the Black Watch, or 42nd Royal Highland Regiment, as they were to become known, were posted to Flanders to take part in the War of the Austrian Succession. Their Colonel, Lt Colonel Sir Robert Munro of Foulis, obtained permission for them to fight in their own way and at Fontenoy in 1745 they excelled. It is recorded:

According to the usage of his countrymen he ordered the regiment to clap to the ground on receiving the French fire. Instantly after its discharge the men sprang up and coming close to the enemy poured their shot upon them to the certain destruction of multitudes and drove them precipitately back through their own lines; then retreating, drew up again and attacked a second time in the same manner. These attacks they repeated several times in the same day to the surprise of the whole army.

In 1745 Prince Charles Edward Stuart, the Young Pretender, made a last desperate bid to restore the Stuarts to the throne. His army at best consisted only of 5,000 men, some of whom were Lowlanders, only raising support in the Highlands from the largely Roman Catholic and Episcopalian Camerons, Stewarts and Macdonalds. Not all of them went willingly or so they claimed when they stood trial for treason. Along Speyside able-bodied men were told that their cottages would be burned if they did not answer Lord Lewis Gordon's demand for recruits. After the rebellion was over the Reverend James Robertson wrote a petition asking mercy for fifteen men of his parish at Lochbroom then lying in prison at Tilbury on the Thames. He said that, in March, Macdonald of Keppoch had come by, snatching men from their bed and dragging them from their ploughs: 'One I did myself see overtaken, and when he declared he would rather die than be carried to rebellion, was knocked to the ground by the butt of a musket and carried away all blood'.

Reluctant or not, Highlanders had always been formidable warriors as shown by the victories in the seventeenth and eighteenth centuries under Montrose, Viscount Dundee, Lord George Murray and Prince Charles Edward Stuart. Up until the end of the sixteenth centuries the arms and armour of the Highland warrior were still medieval. Each Clan formed a regiment with an establishment similar to that used in European armies, except that all the ranks and appointments depended on position in the Clan. The Chief was the Colonel, his eldest son the Lieut.-Colonel, second son a major and so on. Heads of large families were Captains: each family stood together in the ranks, the best armed being in the front. Mobilization was effected by means of relay runners sent out by the Chief, each bearing a burning cross with bloodstained cloth attached and shouting the Clan slogan as he ran.

His armour, if he possessed it, was a long mail shirt; his head was protected by a clogaid, or conical steel cap. His main weapon was a great two-handed sword, the claidheamh mor, or claymore. Other favoured weapons were the Lochaber axe, a long-handled battle axe with a spike on the head, and the dirk, a long dagger for use in close combat. By the seventeenth century, firearms became more common. The claymore was abandoned in favour of a single-edged broadsword and the swordsman carried a targe, a small round shield made of oak boards pegged together, covered in leather and reinforced with metal studs. Lightweight shields and swords made possible the development of the 'Highland Charge', which was used with devastating effect at Killiecrankie, Prestonpans and Falkirk. At Culloden a preliminary artillery bombardment, accurate musket-fire and disciplined bayonet-drill halted the suicidal charge of the half-starved and exhausted Highlanders.

The martial value of the Highlander was recognised by some before the '45 rebellion. Prominent Whig politicians in the Highlands, such as Duncan Forbes of Culloden and the Duke of Argyll, had suggested raising regiments among the Jacobite clans. In 1739 one prophetic commenter at the time observed. 'They [the Highlanders] are a numerous and prolifick People; and, if reformed in their Principles, and Manners, and usefully employ'd, might be made a considerable Accession of Power and Wealth to Great Britain. Some Clans of Highlanders, well instructed in the Arts of War, and well affected to the Government, would make as able and formidable a body for their Country's Defence, as Great Britain, or Switzerland, or any part of Europe was able to produce.' Duncan Forbes agreed and pressed the Government to raise four or five regiments of the line from the clans, 'If Government pre-engage the Highlanders in the manner I propose, they will not only serve well against the enemy abroad, but will be hostages for the good behaviour of their relatives at home, and I am persuaded it will be absolutely impossible to raise a rebellion in the Highlands.'

After the Jacobite Rebellion of 1745, the Duke of Cumberland initially urged mass transportation rather than recruitment of the disaffected to the crown forces, but with Britain's overseas commitments stretching the

Scottish Dragoon of 1680. From History of the Scottish Regiments in the British Army, *Alexander K Murray, 1862.*

domestic supply of recruits, he finally gave his agreement to employing Highland levies. The government in London concluded that the Highlands, unlike Ireland, no longer posed an internal security threat. At the same time, care was taken that the Highland troops did not linger long in Scotland after training but were dispatched overseas with all speed. As a result the Highlanders became the crack troops of imperial warfare, with wide experience in North America, the West Indies and India, encountering long and arduous tours of duty lasting for several years. 'I sought', William Pitt the elder declared 'for merit wherever it was to be found. It is my boast that I was the first Minister who looked for it and found it in the mountains of the north. I called it forth and drew into your service a hardy and intrepid race of men'.

Even after the brutal suppression of the Highlands after the 1745 Rebellion there was no difficulty obtaining recruits. In 1755, when war with France appeared increasingly likely the Black Watch was promptly put on a war-time footing and General Stewart of Garth recorded:

> The Laird of Mackintosh, then a Captain the Regiment, had charge of all the recruiting parties...to the Highlands and quickly collected 500 men, the number he was desired to recruit. Of these he collected 87 men in one forenoon.
> One morning as he was sitting at breakfast in Inverness, 38 men of the name of Macpherson from Badenoch, appeared in front of the window with an offer of their services to Mackintosh; their own immediate chief, the Laird of Cluny, being then in exile, in consequence of hid attainder after the Rising.

In 1757, when the Seven Years War with France finally broke out, numerous other Highland regiments were raised. Stuart went on to note that when the Highland regiments landed in America their appearance attracted much notice. 'The Indians in particular were delighted to see a European regiments so similar to their own.' He quoted a New Yorker who wrote: 'When the Highlanders landed they were caressed by all ranks and orders of men, but more particularly by the Indians. On the march to Albany, the Indians flocked from all quarters to see the strangers, who, they believed, were of the same extraction as themselves, and therefore received them as brothers'. In the conclusion of the war in 1763 all these regiments returned home and were reduced, but those who had served in America were offered the alternative of being given a grant of land and settling in America. Many of them chose to do so and their letters to their friends and relations at home were a potent stimulus to future emigration.

More Highland regiments were hastily raised to fight in America with the outbreak of war in the colonies. The 71st or Fraser's Highlanders, raised in 1775, served at Brooklyn, Savannah and York River. The news of General Burgoryne's disaster at Saratoga, in 1777 led the Duke of Hamilton to raise a regiment of 1000 men on his own estate. Another peer, the Duke of Atholl, also enlisted a regiment among his retainers. Chief Macleod, who had been formerly a strong supporter of Prince Charlie, also founded a regiment, which afterwards became the 1st Highland Light Infantry. The cities of Edinburgh and Glasgow each raised and equipped a Regiment as did the families of Argyll, Gordon, Seaforth and Macdonald; but nearly all of these, after they had done their work in America, were disbanded.

Successful recruitment could provide benefits for the Highland gentry. The Warrant or Beating Order issued by the Secretary of War, permitting the raising of a new corps, authorized the recruitment of officers and men, the numbers involved and the bounties to be paid to recruits. Bounties rose dramatically in the later eighteenth century as the army underwent continued expansion. Official levels for Highland recruits were £3 in 1757 but had spiralled to £21–£30 in 1794. Landlords in the north of Scotland were able to exploit these rising values because rather than paying full bounty money they used land on their estates in return for the supply of recruits. Tenants were expected to supply a family member of a 'purchased man' whose bounty was paid by the tenant himself. Through this mechanism landlords made huge profits which during wartime equalled and sometimes even surpassed the income from agriculture of the estate. If

Major Charles Johnstone. From John Kay, A Series of Original Portraits, With Biographical Sketches and Illustrative Anecdotes. Edinburgh: A C Black, 1877

recruits were not forthcoming from the ranks of the tenantry systematic coercion was employed. Alexander Macdonnel of Glengarry ordered his agent to 'warn out' a list of small tenants from his Knoydart property, they 'having refused to serve me'. Similarly, MacLean of Lochbuie on the island of Mull threatened to remove seventy-one tenants, cottars and their families in 1795 because they had not provided sons for service.

Life as a foot soldier was tough, even when stationed in Scotland as recounted by George Penny, in *Traditions of Perth*, published in 1836:

There being no barracks, the soldiers were all billeted on the inhabitants, and in most cases were wretchedly lodged; often in open tiled garrets with an unglazed window, or in dismal vaults fit only for pigs. – Incredible as it may now appear, this regiment, when in Perth, were under stoppages, which left the men only 3d a day. Their common breakfast was a half-penny roll, and a half-penny worth of Suffolk cheese; and those who sought to alleviate their suffering by taking a glass of spirits, got no more food for twenty-four hours. The consequence was, that these men, from sheer necessity, were frequently driven to commit petty depredations, and as these, when discovered, were followed by punishments quite disproportionate to the office, the North Inch became a scene of continual barbarity. It was no uncommon thing to see six, or even ten, of these unfortunate wretches suffer from 100 to 500 lashes each; and this continued day after day, till sometimes the washerwomen interfered, and, partly by threats and partly by entreaty, succeeded in getting a few of them pardoned.

For those who married soldier life was also one of hardship and sacrifice as can be seen in the Regimental Standing Orders, of the 90th Light Infantry:

No woman is to be allowed to reside in Barracks who objects to make herself useful in Cooking, &c. It cannot be too often repeated to the men that they are on no account to marry without leave. A Man marrying, without having obtained leave from the Commanding Officer of the Regiment, will never be permitted to receive any of the indulgences bestowed on such as marry by consent. It is impossible to point out the inconveniences which arise and the evils which follow a Regiment encumbered with

Women: poverty and misery are the inevitable consequences. Officers therefore cannot do too much to deter their men from marrying; and there are few men, however had they may think it at the moment, that after a short period, will not be obliged to them for having done so.

Women who left home to marry soldiers could find themselves shunned by their neighbours as James Anton recalled in his *Retrospect of A Military Life,* published in 1841: 'In a small closet adjoining that which we were to occupy, lodged three unfortunate girls, lately arrived from Hamilton, from which place they had been induced (by promises of marriage) to follow their lovers, not stationed near Edinburgh. These poor girls, after being drawn so far from home, were disappointed, and they now felt ashamed to return.'

Between 1740 and 1815 no fewer than fifty battalions of the line, three of service and seven of militia were raised in the Highlands, in addition to twenty-six regiments of fencibles – regular troops embodied for the duration of a war. By the later 1790s, however, the manpower resources of the region were virtually exhausted, not only because of over-recruitment but also death in battle, disease, discharges and natural attrition. Even the most prestigious regiments were forced to extend their territorial range of recruitment. At least a third of the Black Watch who fought at Waterloo were drawn from the Lowlands, the Borders and England. By the Victorian period Highland regiments comprised only a minority of Highlanders as mass emigration took its toll on the region, especially after the Great Famine of the 1840s which preceded the Crimean War by only a few years. As Lord Selkirk lamented as early as 1805:

This change in the character and composition of the Highland regiments, is not a mere speculative probability, but has been actually going on in a progressive manner, ever since the advance of rents began to be considerable. We must go back to the seven-years war to find these regiments in their original purity, formed entirely on the feudal principle, and raised in the manner that has been described. Even as early as the American war, some tendency towards a different system was to be observed; and during the late war, it went so far, that many regiments were Highland scarcely more than in name. Some corps were indeed composed nearly in the ancient manner; but there were others in which few of the men had any connexion whatever with the estates of their officers, being recruited, in the ordinary manner, in Glasgow and other manufacturing places, and consisting of any description of people, Lowlanders and Irish, as well as Highlanders.

The last of the regular Highland regiments to come on the scene was the 93rd Sutherland Highlanders raised in 1800. The method of recruitment used was based on the ancient feudal system. First a census was made of all suitable men on the estates of the Countess of Sutherland and notice went round that a proportion of them would be expected to do their duty to their Chief and to the King, by enlisting. Major-General William Wemyss then held a meeting in each parish at which the eligible men were lined up for his inspection. Passing along the ranks, snuff-box in hand, followed by a gillie bearing a supply of whisky, he offered snuff to each man who took his fancy. The selected recruit took a pace forward, received his snuff and his dram while the clerk entered his name.

This approach, very similar to one of the old Clan regiments, encouraged fierce loyalty as outlined in *The 93rd Digest of Service*, 1800:

Officers of the Hopetoun Fencibles. From John Kay, A Series of Original Portraits, With Biographical Sketches and Illustrative Anecdotes. Edinburgh: A C Black, 1877

For in such a regiment not only did each individual feel accountable for his own character, but in some degree for the conduct of his comrades; and as, in order to increase wholesome rivalship between the different Companies of the Battalion, they were at first classified by parishes, an arrangement which naturally excited the greatest emulation, it followed that every soldier became speedily convinced that by behaving ill he should not only be covered with personal disgrace, but would in some measure bring dishonour to the parish to which he, in common with all his comrades in the same Company with himself, belonged.

Highland Regiments stood out from other regiments of the line by their traditional costume. In 1804 when the British government contemplated doing away with the kilt and issuing standard uniforms to their Scottish troops, there was a massive uproar. An exasperated Colonel Alan Cameron of the 79th Camerons passionately defended the feileadhbeag and its 'free congenial circulation of pure wholesome air (as an exhilarating native bracer) which has hitherto so peculiarly benefitted the Highlander for activity, and all the other necessary qualities of a soldier, whether for hardship under scanty fare, readiness in accounting, or making forced marches' and concluded: 'I sincerely hope His Royal Highness will never acquiesce in so painful and degrading an idea (come from whatever quarter it may) as to strip us of our native garb ... and stuff us in breeches'. Whitehall dropped the idea.

By the French Revolutionary and Napoleonic Wars the number of recruits, now drawn increasingly from the Scottish Lowlands was unprecedented. The most recent careful estimate suggests totals ranging from 37,000 to 48,000 men in regular, fencible and Volunteer units. The heroic actions of the Highland regiments in the Napoleonic wars caught the imagination of the country. When they returned these regiments were disbanded, or reduced to peace-time requirements. A writer in the south, who had seen them marching past, wrote using the pseudonym 'Near Observer': 'On many a Highland hill and Lowland valley long will the deeds of these men be remembered'. General Stewart of Garth felt compelled to note that many of these men returned to their traditional lands to find that most of the inhabitants had been replaced with sheep. 'This 'Near Observer' perhaps did not know that, on many a Highland hill, and in many a Highland glen, few are left to mourn the death, or rejoice over the deeds of the departed brave. New views of Highland statistic have changed the birth-place of many a brave soldier and defender of the honour, prosperity and independence of this country, to a desolate waste, where no maimed soldier can now find a home, or shelter, and where the sounds of the pipes and the voice of innocent gaiety and happiness are no longer heard'.

The Highland clearances had changed everything. During the Crimean War the government's appeal for troops met with an angry response. At one meeting a spokesman told the landlords to 'Send your deer, your roes, your rams, dogs, shepherds and game-keepers to fight the Russians. They have never done us any harm'. The Duke of Sutherland sent agent James Loch to recruit his tenants. He toured the country for six weeks with no success. The indignant Duke called a meeting of all the male inhabitants in the parishes of Clyne, Rogart and Golspie and offered a bounty of £6 of every man who enlisted in the 93rd or £3 if he enlisted in some other corps. His offer was greeted with silence. When he asked for an explanation and old man told him:

It is the opinion of this country that should the Czar of Russia take possession of Dunrobin Castle and of Stafford House next term that we couldn't expect worse treatment at his hands than we have experienced in the hands of your family for the last fifty years ... How could you expect to find men where they are not, and the few of them which are to be found among the rubbish or ruins of the country have more sense than to be decoyed by chaff to the field of slaughter. But one comfort you have. Though you cannot find men to fight, you can supply those who will fight with plenty of mutton, beef and venison.

As the war continued so did the evictions. Some disbanded men of the 93rd came home to the parish of Lairg to find that a factor known to them as Domhnal Sgrios, Donald Destruction, had cleared their families and pulled down their houses. They caught him at his work, striped him naked and beat him with switches of gorse.

During the Crimean War the Highland Regiments, containing an increasing numbers of recruits from the manufacturing towns, distinguished themselves again. The 42nd or Black Watch, the 79th or Cameron Highlanders, and 93rd or Sutherland Highlanders were brigaded together in a single Highland Brigade under General Colin Campbell, later Lord Clyde.

Piper Muir of the 42nd (Royal Highlanders) after his return from the Crimea, 1856. National Museums of Scotland

At the Battle of Alma on 20 September 1854, the three Highland battalions were given the task of protecting the left flank of the British army. As his men waited under fire and as casualties mounted, Campbell addressed them:

> Now, men, you are going into action. Remember this: whoever is wounded – I don't care what his rank is – whoever is wounded must lie where he falls till the bandsmen come to attend him. No soldiers must go carrying off wounded men. If any soldier does such a thing, his name shall be struck up in his parish church. Don't be in a hurry about firing. Your officers will tell you when it is time to open fire. Be steady. Keep silence, fire low. Now men, the army will watch us; make me proud of the Highland Brigade!

They not only overcame and put to flight eight Russian battalions, the pick of the Russian army, but caused four more to retreat.

On 25 October in the same year, the 93rd Highlanders covered themselves in glory at the Battle of Balaclava. In the words of Surgeon General William Munro, who was with them:

A considerable body of horse wheeling south advanced in our direction at a brisk pace…which gradually increased to a gallop…The Turkish battalions on our flanks…broke and bolted. It was at this moment that Sir Colin Campbell rode along the front of the 93rd telling the Regiment to be 'Steady!' for if necessary every man would have 'to die where he stood' He was answered by the universal and cheery response, 'Ay, ay, Sir Colin, need's be, we'll do that'.

In the event the 93rd spread out only two deep, with bayonets fixed, stood firm to the admiration of all who witnessed the battle. The cavalry, faced with two devastating volleys at close range, swerved away and galloped back to their lines in full retreat. In the words of a war correspondent the 93rd were, 'The thin red streak, tipped with a line of steel', – thereafter more frequently known as the 'Thin Red Line'. They were the only infantry regiment to have the word Balaclava on their battle honours. At the end of the war the Highland Brigade was transferred direct to India in 1857 on the outbreak of the Indian Mutiny once again under Sir Colin Campbell. At the relief of Lucknow alone, the 42nd Black Watch and the 93rd Sutherland Highlanders between them gained fifteen VCs.

By the end of the nineteenth century there were no longer sufficient recruits in the Highlands. By the simple process of amalgamation the Highland Regiments were reduced to six, allowing each a selected recruiting area to which it had to adhere. Thus the remnants of the eighty-six Highland regiments which had been recruited between 1730 and 1815 became the Black Watch, the Gordons, the Seaforths, the Camerons, the Highland Light Infantry, and the Argyll and Sutherlands. These regiments served with distinction in many Imperial Wars throughout the nineteenth and twentieth centuries making a disproportionate contribution to the British armed services. Over 100,000, for example, were killed in the First World War. 'Pals' battalions', such as those of the Highland Light Infantry which recruited mainly from Glasgow slums, were formed almost overnight from particular localities or the workplace: another battalion in the same regiment was entirely made up, in the space of sixteen hours, of the employers of Glasgow Corporation tramways.

No more moving example of the continued bravery of the Scottish soldier was demonstrated by the extraordinary response made by the Hearts players to the call for recruits in 1914. Every member of the team joined a new battalion being promoted in Edinburgh by Lieutenant-Colonel Sir George McCrae. On 26 November 1914, *The Times* carried the headline 'ELEVEN LEADING PLAYERS ENLISTED'. The 'Football Sensation' captured the country's imagination: McCrae's Battalion (the 16th Royal Scots) was raised in record time. The example of the Tynecastle men was followed at once by around 500 of their supporters and ticket-holders – along with 150 followers of their deadly rivals Hibernian. Other professionals volunteered including those from Raith Rovers, Falkirk and Dunfermline. In total, around 75 local clubs (of all levels) were represented – along with rugby players, hockey players, strongmen, golfers, bowlers and athletes of all persuasions.

McCrae's crossed to France in 1916; on 1 July they took part in the infamous opening day of the Battle of the Somme. They were selected to assault the most dangerous part of the enemy position, a fearsome network of barbed wire and entrenchments, bristling with machine-guns. In spite of this, they took every objective and achieved the deepest penetration of the German line anywhere on the front that morning. In the process they lost three-quarters of their strength. Three of the Hearts' players, Harry Wattie, Duncan Currie and Ernie Ellis, were killed. Another member of the team, twenty-two-year-old Paddy Crossan, was so badly injured that his right leg was labelled for amputation. He pleaded with the German surgeon not to operate. He told him: 'I need my legs – I'm a footballer.' He agreed to his request and managed to save his leg. Crossan survived the war but later died as a result of his lungs being destroyed by poison gas. By the end of the war seven members of the Hearts team had been killed in action.

Chapter Nine

MIGRATION AND EMIGRATION

D r Johnson once observed that 'the noblest prospect which a Scotchman ever sees, is the high road that leads him to England'. By the end of the eighteenth century, Scots from both the Highlands and Lowlands were heading for the rapidly expanding industrial towns of southern Scotland and travelling south to England in ever increasing numbers where they would have a disproportionately large influence in their adopted country as writers, doctors, engineers and politicians.

In Scotland itself, early records of migration usually chronicled exceptional movements of people, such as the scheme of James VI to settled Lowlanders in Kintyre, Lochabir and Lewis. One of the most significant migrations from Scotland occurred during the seventeenth century and it was to have a lasting impact on the history of their adopted country. The Flight of the Earls in 1607 offered James VI an opportunity to settle Lowland Scots in Ulster. Fifty-nine Scottish undertakers were allotted land and each was accompanied to his new home by kinsmen, friends, and tenants, as Lord Ochiltree, for instance, who is mentioned as having arrived 'accompanied with thirty-three followers, a minister, some tenants, freeholders, [and] artificers.' The vast majority of the Scottish undertakers came from the central lowland belt, especially the Edinburgh/Haddington area in the east and the Renfrew/north Ayrshire area in the west. Apart from a few from the east coast of Scotland north of Fife, the only other area from which significant numbers were drawn was the extreme south-west of the country between Dumfries and Portpatrick. Surviving records suggest that Tyrone and Fermanagh attracted relatively large numbers of settlers from the Border counties. The most common surnames were Johnson, Armstrong, Elliot, Graham and Beatty.

Unknown Scottish Ancestor. Author's collection

By the end of 1612 the emigration from Scotland is estimated to have reached 10,000. New waves of migration occurred throughout the seventeenth century and by the 1640s, the settler population in Ulster had swelled to some 40,000. Sir William Brereton, an Englishman travelling through Ayrshire in 1634, wrote: 'Above ten thousand persons have, within two last years past, left the country wherein they lived ... and are gone for Ireland. They have come by one hundred in company through the town, and three hundred have gone on hence together, shipped for Ireland at one tide ... Their swarming in Ireland is so much taken notice of and disliked, as that the Deputy hath sent out a warrant to stay the landing of any of these Scotch that came without a certificate'. Although many Sots were killed or driven out during the Irish rebellion of 1641 their numbers were more than replenished by later waves of immigration, particularly after the Williamite victory of 1690. These new migrants were attracted by the offer of farms that had been laid waste during the recent war. Archbishop Synge, the Anglican divine, in 1715 estimated that fifty thousand Scots had come to Ulster between 1690 and 1700.

By the eighteenth century changing agricultural practices and the rapid growth of the towns and cities encouraged migration on an ever increasing scale. Until the eighteenth century, most migrants travelled little more than ten miles. Many were farm servants who were employed on six months or one year contracts, and they rarely stayed at a farm very long before moving to another employer. Despite the creation of larger farmers with more substantial tenants, work on the farms remained labour intensive and workers were still required. During busy seasons such as harvest, farmers still relied on temporary migrants, not only from the Lowlands but in increasing numbers from the Highlands.

By the second half of the nineteenth century the population of the Scottish Highlands was declining rapidly. Like their counterparts in the Lowlands they left their native parishes as agricultural changes forced them off the land towards the opportunities and uncertainties of city life. Highland migrants often followed other locals or fellow parishioners to cities such as Glasgow where they settled in them same areas. The proportion of Argyll-born Highlanders in Shettleston and Maryhill, for example, was higher than for the city as a whole and large numbers of migrants from Bute settled in St John's parish. The Rev Dr Norman Macleod to the Poor Law Commissioners confirmed this:

> I think the Highlanders find it more easy to get respectable employment than the Irish; the Highlanders have many friends in Glasgow to whom they can apply. They come with letters of recommendation to countrymen and clansmen who are in comfortable circumstances; we are very clannish; and those who come from one Ireland do it for the men from that Island who have to get employment – the Macdonalds for the Macdonalds and the Macleods for the Macleods and so on, so that they find very little difficulty in getting work.

The Highlanders worked in a variety of jobs in the Lowland towns and cities. In 1791 Thomas Newte commented: 'As the offices of drudgery, and of labour, that require not any skill, are generally performed in London by Irishmen, and Welsh people of both sexes, so all such inferior departments are filled in Edinburgh by the Highlanders'. In the capital, 'as well as other cities of note in Scotland', there was a constant influx [of Highlanders] 'to supply the places of porters, barrowmen, chairmen and such like'. However, there is a great deal of evidence to show that they many Highlanders were employed in skilled occupations such as printing, coopering, inn-keeping and in textiles. In Glasgow, for example, several Highlanders became prominent industrialists: Robert Macfie in Greenock's sugar refinery and Archibald Campbell in the glassworks there in 1793. Probably the most notable was George Macintosh who, by 1777, had established the Dunchatten dye works at Dennistoun, on the north-east outskirts of Glasgow. All the employers were Highlanders and a role call was taken in Gaelic every morning. In 1841, one commentator observed:

> There are very few jobs in Glasgow in which Highlanders are not found: the classes who have received the benefit of education are employed in warehouses; they are employed as clerks, and so on: the other classes, the uneducated, are employed at various public works.

For both Highlanders and rural Lowlanders, the burgeoning industrial towns in England provided the main stimulus to migrate further south, thanks to higher wages and the perception of better conditions than in farming or crafting. These migrants were following a well-worn path. Scots had being heading south as seasonal migrants in Cumberland as early as the fifteenth century. In the mid-fifteenth century there were up to 11,000 Scots in England, coming mainly from eastern Scotland and settling primarily in Northumberland if they were unskilled and London if they were skilled tradesmen or professional men. The Union of 1707 obviously created new opportunities for Scots; it certainly encouraged the nobility to move south and probably made England a generally more attractive emigration destination. Daniel Defoe, on his extensive travels around Britain in the 1720s noted the strong Scottish presence particularly in the north of England:

> ...you have in England abundance of Scotsmen, Scots costumes, words, habits, and usages, even more than becomes them; nay, even the buildings in the towns, and in the villages, imitate the Scots almost all over Northumberland; witness their building the houses with the stairs (to the second floor) going up on the outside of the house, so that one family may live below, and another above, without going in at the same door; which is the Scots way of living, and which we see in Alnwick and Warkworth, and several other

towns; witness also their setting their corn up in great numbers in small stacks without doors, not making use of any barns, only a particular building, which they call a barn, but, which is itself no more than a threshing-floor into which they take one of those small stacks at a time, and thresh it out, and then take in another; which we have great reason to believe was the usage of the antients,[sic] seeing we read of threshing-floors often; but very seldom, of a barn, except that of the rich glutton.

Between 1830 and 1914, an estimated 600,000 Scots trekked south. It is difficult to assess the numbers heading to England, since the country of birth of Scottish immigrants was not stated in the English census until 1911. By that time a new type of migrant was travelling south of the border. A feature of most successful English teams of the 1880s and 1890s was the number of Scottish football players. The Lancashire clubs in particular

Parliament House. From James Grant, Old & New Edinburgh, *issued in weekly instalments c.1890.*

actively recruited in Scotland and the Scottish press carried many advertisements of jobs available in Blackburn, Burnley and other cotton towns for men with footballing talent. These 'Scotch professors' owed their reputation to their commitment to winning and their skill at the passing game, rather than the 'kick and rush' or individual dribbling styles favoured in England. Bolton, Darwen, and Preston included many Scottish players, and the first Liverpool of 1892, did not contain a single English player, quickly becoming known as the 'team of the macs'.

By the end of the eighteenth century, Scottish migration to Ireland had been reduced to a trickle. Irish immigrants, on the other hand, established a strong presence in Scotland. Between 1790 and 1850, over 300,000 Irish men, women and children arrived in Scotland. Some came for seasonal employment. In the 1820s, 6,000–8,000 Irish a year were making the harvest migration and by the 1840s this had grown to 25,000 over the agricultural season. The number of Irish immigrants rose dramatically during the Great Famine when, in the late 1840's the potato crop failed over the whole of Ireland, and that failure was repeated in successive years. Many starving and destitute people fled to the industrial towns, particularly in the west of Scotland. The *Glasgow Herald* described it in June 1847 as 'The Irish Invasion' and complained that: 'The streets of Glasgow are at present literally swarming with vagrants from the sister kingdom, and the misery which many of these poor creatures endure can scarcely be less than what they have fled or been driven from at home. Many of them are absolutely without procuring lodging of even the meanest description, and are obliged consequently to make their bed frequently with a stone for a pillow'. Such has been the impact of the Irish community in Scotland that many surnames such as Docherty, Gallagher and Murphy became so common in Scotland as to have become naturalised.

For centuries before the exodus to the New World, Scots had been emigrating to mainland Europe as merchants and soldiers. Many emigrated to France, Poland, Italy and Holland. As early as 1616 William Lithgow, the noted Scots traveller, termed Poland the 'mother and nurse of the youths and younglings of Scotland, clothing, feeding and enriching them with the fatness of their best things, besides 30,000 Scots families that live incorporate in her bowels'. Many of these Scottish came from Dundee and Aberdeen and could be found in Polish towns from Krakow to Lubin. The Scots integrated well and many acquired great wealth. Some of the corruption of Scottish names which arose in Poland and East Prussia at this time are interesting. In

Warsaw some typical corruptions noted in various documents were Chalmers to Czamer, Drew to Driowsky, Weir to Wier, Soutar to Zutter, Scott to Zlot, Brown to Burn, Macallan to Makalienski, Wright to Rytt, and Ross to Rusek. In Prussia the corruptions noted were Arnott to Ahrnett, Auld to Altt, Polwarth to Bollwarth, Forbes to Ferbrus, Douglas to Doglass and Cumming to Konig.

Scottish merchants had established strong ties in the colonies by the end of the seventeenth century. They penetrated the Chesapeake Bay and the Hames, Potomac and Delaware Rivers, and operated as far north as Boston. Scottish settlers started arriving as early as the 1680s and, as Britain's role in North America expanded, the Scottish presence grew with it. The bitter persecution of Presbyterians during the periods of Episcopal rule in the latter half of the seventeenth century provided a powerful incentive for many to emigrate to the New World in search of religious toleration.

For the majority of emigrants, America offered both an escape route from poverty and persecution and an opportunity for advancement for the ambitious and adventurous. The Union of England and Scotland in 1707 removed all restrictions on Scottish trade with the English colonies and soon Glasgow virtually monopolised the Tobacco trade with the Chesapeake. This, too, led to further settlement in America. Within a generation Glasgow and Greenock became two of the most prominent ports in British intercontinental trade, soon becoming the main exit ports for Scots migrants.

By the early eighteenth century Scottish settlements were established in the Savannah area of Georgia and around Cape Fear in North Carolina. Many were refugees from the 1745 rebellion: MacLeods, MacDonalds, MacRaes, MacDougalls and Campbells found themselves in a land where their native Gaelic isolated them even from their Scottish neighbours. This is where Allan and Flora MacDonald and her husband would settle when they came to America. It is a remarkable fact during the American War of Independence these Highlanders tended to rally to the British colours. Immediately upon the outbreak of war MacDonald offered his services to the loyalist side and was appointed second-in-command of the loyalist militia raised from the Highlanders in the Cape Fear region.

When the war ended many Scots would end up paying for their support of the British government by having to leave, as the newly independent Americans made it clear that they were no longer welcome. Allan and Flora MacDonald returned to their original home, on the Isle of Skye. One hundred and fifty thousand other Loyalist exiles, at least a fifth of them

St John's, Castlehill. From James Grant, Old & New Edinburgh, *issued in weekly instalments c.1890.*

Scots, left for the remaining British dominions in the Americas. At least a half went to Canada, and nearly 35,000 of those to Nova Scotia. After the opulence of life in the thirteen colonies, immigrants found conditions there austere: some nicknamed their new home 'Nova Scarcity'.

The American Revolution War led to a lull in emigration from Scotland, but by the nineteenth century the United States was once again the most popular destination for Scottish emigrants. Some chose to emigrate in order to avoid imprisonment at home. In 1833 a committee was appointed in Aberdeen to tackle the problem of debtors resorting to emigration in order to escape their creditors. The Minister for the Dumfriesshire parish of Hutton and Corrie complained in the *New Statistical Account*:

> Much loss and mischief are occasioned by dishonest emigrants to America. It is well-known, that the United States and the North American British Colonies are the quarters to which the eyes of thousands, who find they cannot thrive in their own country, are anxiously directed. And of these a considerable proportion are

guilty of dishonest practices. During the ministry of the present incumbent, not much short of a score have left this parish under charges of various kinds; some to avoid supporting illegitimate children, – some, after swindling practices and committing forgery, – and some after committing frauds of all sorts, with a view to emigrate with their ill-gotten gains. The state of our North American colonies is such, that it may be said to hold out a premium to the practice of villainy in the mother country.

For those in the Scottish towns with skills, emigration offered higher wages and better working conditions especially in the factories, mines and workshops of the United States. Throughout the 1850s and 1860s Scottish coal-miners emigrated in large numbers and were to be found in Maryland and Pennsylvania, and as far west as Illinois and Ohio. Wages were so high that quite a number of miners found it profitable enough to work the summer months in America, either working their sea-passage each way or travelling steerage. There were also large communities of Scottish stonemasons in Maine, New Hampshire and Massachusetts and by the 1860s, after the Scottish cotton industry had suffered a severe recession, Scottish workers emigrated to America where they earned nearly double their wages. From the 1820s, emigrants from Paisley and Kilmarnock flocked to the carpet-manufacturing centres of Lowell, Massachusetts, and Thompsonville, Connecticut, while the workers brought out to Newark, New Jersey, and Pawtucket and Fall River, Massachusetts, by the Paisley thread-making firms of Clark, J&P. Coats and Kerr, earned double the wages they had been paid in Scotland.

According to the 1790 census there were 189,000 people of Scottish origin in the United States although this may include many of Scottish descent who had emigrated from Ulster. During the second great wave of emigration, between 1861 and 1901, more than 500,000 Scots emigrated to the United States. The greatest numbers were to be found in the mid-Atlantic states, New York, Pennsylvania and Massachusetts in that order. Following them were the east north-central states (Illinois, Michigan and Ohio) and the Pacific coasts states, most notably California. Those attracted to the cities were to be found mostly in New York, Chicago, Philadelphia and Detroit.

Canada from the beginning its history is closely associated with Scotsmen. French and Scottish fishermen were making rich hauls off the coast of Newfoundland and Labrador as early as 1506; and these fishermen, together with adventurers and fur traders pushed their way up the St. Lawrence to Quebec and Montreal. In 1621 Sir William Alexander, a favourite of James I was given vast tracts of land in Cape Breton, Prince Edward Island, and New Brunswick, as well as parts of Vermont, New Hampshire, Maine and Quebec. With the idea of founding a New Scotland, or Nova Scotia, he attempted for form a settlement. The first settlers left Scotland in 1622 and arrived in Nova Scotia in the autumn. They survived the winter with some losses and were relieved by a second ship in 1623, but nothing was achieved in the way of a permanent settlement. Subsequent attempts to revive the scheme also ended in failure.

Scots would, nevertheless, play a leading role in the conquest of Canadian territories over the next two centuries. They made an important contribution to the successful outcome of the Seven Years War between France and England which began in 1756. One of the most memorable events in the war took place in 1759 when General James Wolfe led the Highlanders in a surprise attack on Quebec, where on the Fields of Abraham the French were defeated and the city captured. Fraser's Highlanders was the largest regiment on the Plains of Abraham and suffered the heaviest casualties. According to Dr Robert Macpherson who witnessed the battle:

The Highlanders pursued them to the very Sally Port of the town. The Highlanders returned towards the main body. When the highlanders were gathered together, they lay'd on a separate attack against a large body of Canadians on our flank that were posted in a small village and a Bush of woods.Here, after a wonderfull escape all day, we suffered great loss both in Officers and men but at last drove them under the cover of their cannon which likeways did us considerable loss.

After 1763, Fraser's Highlanders were disbanded and many settled in Quebec and the Maritime Provinces. Notable among these settlements was that of Malcolm Fraser and Major Nairn at Murray Bay. It was from these soldier settlements that Colonel Allan Maclean, in 1775, raised his Royal Highland Emigrants, who garrisoned Quebec against invasion during the American War of the Revolution.

After the American Revolution Canada was increasingly favoured by Scots from both the Highlands and Lowlands. Most of the early Scots

Loch Scavig, Skye. From William Daniell, Voyage Round Great Britain, *1820.*

settlers chose one of the maritime provinces – Nova Scotia, Cape Breton Island or Prince Edward Island – but others found their way inland to Upper Canada (Ontario). Ontario was also almost exclusively a Scottish colony, settled by Highland families who came over from New York State during and after the American Revolution and disbanded soldiers from the frontier regiments organized by Sir John Johnson. Most numerous of these were Macdonells, from Glengarry and Inverness, with Camerons, Chisholms, Fergusons, Grants, MacIntyres, and others, who cleared what was once wilderness and is now represented by the present counties of Glengarry, Stormont and Dundas. In 1785 alone , more than 500, almost the entire parish of Knoydart, Glengarry, emigrated direct from Scotland and settled in a body in Ontario.

By August 1849 *The Scotsman* claimed that 20,000 highlanders had emigrated to Canada during the previous decade, a tally that increased in the early 1850s as Outer Hebridean landowners in particular responded to persistent famine with intensified subsidised emigration programmes. Canada's chief immigration agent, Alexander Buchanan, was scathing in his condemnation of the deliberately inadequate provision made by some landlords who, having chosen Canada for its proximity and cheap access, despatched maximum numbers of emigrants at minimum cost and expected his department to foot the bill for onward travel from the port of landing. But greater opprobrium was heaped on infamous evictors, particularly John Gordon, for the brutal recruitment techniques allegedly used in rounding up emigrants from his estates in Barra and South Uist. Fifteen hundred people from Gordon's estates went to Canada, many of them paupers who needed support from the colony. They went to Upper Canada, where the *Dundas Warder* reported their arrival with indignation:

> We have been pained beyond measure for some time to witness in our streets so may unfortunate Highland emigrants, many of them sick from want and other attendant causes ... There will be many to sound the fulsome noise of flattery in the ear of a generous landlord who had spent so much to assist the emigration of his poor tenants. They will give him the misnomer of benefactor, and for what? Because he rid his estates of the encumbrance of a pauper population.

Mount Stuart, Isle of Bute. William Daniell, Voyage Round Great Britain, *1820.*

These Highlanders tended to form settlements with their fellow countrymen and built up Gaelic-speaking enclaves in Cape Breton Island, the Eastern Townships of Quebec, Glengarry, and the prairie colonies of Killarney and Benbecula.

By 1856 the Canada, Australia and New Zealand were vying with each other to attract emigrants. Significant numbers of Scottish people had already settled in Australia.

The streets of the South Island city of Dunedin founded in 1848 were named after the Scottish capital by a group of members of the Free Church of Scotland, including the Rev. Thomas Burns, the nephew of the poet. There is therefore a Princes Street, George Street, St Andrew's Street, Moray Place and Heriot Row and even a Canongate Street.

In the extreme south of the South Island the town of Invercargill was founded in 1857. That same year, 2,000 emigrants sailed from Scotland in eight ships thanks largely to the promotion work of James Adam an emigration agent one of the original settlers of 1839. Many years later, in 1876, he wrote his memoirs, *Twenty-Five Years of an Emigrant's Life in New Zealand*. He recorded:

> ... Wearisome as eighty days sailing to New Zealand may appear in comparison with ten or twenty to America, yet I question if the advantages to the emigrant are not greater in the one case than in the other. The long voyage teaches the emigrant patience and economy in stowing himself and family afterwards in a small house. Habits of discipline are formed and the art of making the most of everything so that when he lands in his adopted country he is not easily put out with every little annoyance but on the contrary his long passage has only fitted and nerved him for difficulties yet to come...

The influence of the Scots in New Zealand can be seen in many parts of South Island which have Scottish names including Little Paisley, Campbelltown, Oban, Roxburgh and Stirling. Mountains include Ben Nevis, Ben Lomond and Ben More. Like Australian emigrants they kept their Scottish heritage alive and in the First World War the New Zealand Scottish Regiments served with distinction.

It has often been said that Scotland's greatest export was its people, and an estimated 30 million people around the world can claim Scottish descent.

The success of this diaspora world-wide is seen in the annual Tartan Day which is celebrated in Canada, France, Argentina and many more countries. One of the biggest of these celebrations is Tartan Week in New York where Americans with Scottish ancestry throng to the city to celebrate their proud history. In April 2008 President George Bush when he proclaimed 6 April 2008 National Tartan Day, declared:

> Americans of Scottish descent have made enduring contributions to our Nation with their hard work, faith, and values. On National Tartan Day, we celebrate the spirit and character of Scottish Americans and recognize their many contributions to our culture and our way of life.
>
> Scotland and the United States have long shared ties of family and friendship, and many of our country's most cherished customs and ideals first grew to maturity on Scotland's soil. The Declaration of Arbroath, the Scottish Declaration of Independence signed in 1320, embodied the Scots' strong dedication to liberty, and the Scots brought that tradition of freedom with them to the New World. Sons and daughters of many Scottish clans were among the first immigrants to settle in America, and their determination and optimism helped build our Nation's character. Several of our Founding Fathers were of Scottish descent, as have been many Presidents and Justices of the United States Supreme Court. Many Scottish Americans, such as Andrew Carnegie, were great philanthropists, founding and supporting numerous scientific, educational, and civic institutions. From the evocative sounds of the bagpipes to the great sport of golf, the Scots have also left an indelible mark on American culture.

RESEARCH GUIDE

Where to Start

Once bitten by the need to trace your family tree it is very tempting to rush to the nearest archival institution and to be put off immediately by the daunting amount of information available. It is therefore best to start your research at home. Begin with yourself, work through your parents to your grandparents and take each generation as you find it.

Searching through old records, although often rewarding, is often perplexing and frustrating. Even the most experienced researcher can take a wrong turn and end up spending valuable time ploughing through records that only lead to a dead-end. To make more productive use of your time, it is essential to gather as much information as possible from old family Bibles, legal documents (such as wills or leases), and inscriptions from family gravestones. This can help to pinpoint exactly where your family lived at a particular time and provide vital clues to add to names that family historians are often disappointed to find are all too popular in Scotland.

A walk around a graveyard can often save wading through endless pages of a church register for the birth or death dates of a particular ancestor. As well as the names and birth and death dates of particular ancestors, other valuable information can include the deceased's occupation or place of origin and even include the names of husbands, wives or children. They may reveal the married names of daughters or sisters of your ancestors and may record two, three or more generations of a family.

You should treat the information on a headstone (especially ages) with some care. A memorial may refer to two or more people and it may have been placed there on the death of the last person, perhaps many years after the death of the first person buried in the plot.

A death certificate does not indicate the place or date of burial, but your relatives may hold memorial or funeral cards. Because so many headstones can be illegible it is worth checking at your local library to find out if the gravestones in a particular cemetery have been transcribed and published.

If you are interested in finding gravestone inscriptions for your ancestors, you should consult the National Library of Scotland's collection of published monumental inscriptions. The NLS holds an index of monumental inscriptions and a small selection of published volumes of monumental inscriptions in the General Reading Room.

A great deal of work has been done to record inscriptions and the Scottish Genealogical Society has published many of them. They have produced *a list of published & unpublished monumental inscriptions held by the Scottish Genealogy Society* by Angus Mitchell, Mary Mitchell and Marjorie Stewart.

Others are produced by various local history and genealogical societies so it is worth checking out their websites for details. It is important to remember, however, that many mistakes have been made in transcribing inscriptions including omissions and misreadings of hard to decipher headstones. So, if it is at all possible, visit the graveyard where your ancestors are buried.

Be methodical and carefully document your findings. Avoid odd scraps of paper and never depend on your memory however prodigious it may be. You may need to refer back to some piece of research which did not seem promising at the time. If you find some valuable information in a reference book, make sure you keep a reference detailed enough to help you relocate it some years later. This is especially important if you plan to publish your research. Once you have gathered as much information as you can find, particularly names, dates and places it is time to tap into Scotland's rich archival heritage.

Census Records

Census records are an obvious place to begin your archival research. These records provide invaluable information about family relationships, ages, how they earned their livings, and where they were born. Used together with birth, death and marriage records, they enable the family historian to build a very detailed picture of several generations of ancestors. They can also act as a bridge between birth, death and marriage records and the pre-1855 parish registers.

The census records will give you details of those members of the family who lived in a particular address at the time. They will provide you with the age of each member of the family providing you with an important clue to their year of birth which can be followed up in the registration of births. It is important to remember, however, that ages are not always given correctly on census returns. One enumerator commented: 'I may also observe that in a vast number of cases the ladies have understated their ages by from 5–10 years or in some cases 20 years'.

You may also find that someone is missing from the census return that is known to have been alive at the time. In the case of children, for example, they may have been living with another relative. It is possible than an ancestor was working in some other part of the country on census night, or detained at Her Majesty's pleasure. To add to the confusion a child may have died in its infancy and a younger child given the Christian name of the deceased sibling. What appears to be a mistake in the Christian name of a wife may signify the death of the first wife and a second marriage.

There has been a census held in Scotland every ten years since 1801 (excluding 1941) but only those returns after 1841 (with a few earlier exceptions) carry details of named residents. The census enumerator would distribute forms to be filled in on census night, and then go from door to door collecting the completed forms: the accuracy of the information is therefore highly dependent upon the head of the household who completed the form. The forms (which were subsequently destroyed) were copied into the enumerator's book, and it is these for 1841 to 1901 that are available to researchers in a variety of locations.

Census returns for 1841–1901 can be consulted at the General Register Office in Edinburgh and copies on microfilm may be consulted in LDS Family History Centres around the world. The next census to be released is 1911 which will become available on 1st January 2012.

Computerized indexes for the 1841–1901 censuses are available at the General Register Office in Edinburgh, and online at www.scotlands people.gov.uk. Images are also available for 1841 and 1901 and these can be accessed for a fee. The census image is a digital image of a double page of the original enumeration book, showing the members of the household in which you are interested, on census night

Birth, Death and Marriage Records

Registration of births, marriages and deaths began in Scotland on 1 January 1855. Certificates generally give more information than their English counterparts e.g. death certificates name the parents of the deceased, and marriage certificates name mothers as well as fathers of the couple.

Scotland's registration districts were based on existing parish boundaries. All births had to be registered within twenty days, marriages within three days and deaths within eight days. The local registrars kept their own records, but copies were sent to the GROS in Edinburgh, where full indexes were compiled from them all.

Birth records

Birth records include the date and time of birth; address of where the child was born; gender; father's name and occupation; mother's name and maiden name; date of registration; informant's name and relationship (if any) to the child. Birth records for 1855 show parents' ages and places of birth, the date and place of the parents' marriage, the number and gender of any children they had already, and whether any of their children had died.

Marriage records

Until 1929 (when the minimum age was raised to sixteen) boys could marry at fourteen and girls at twelve provided they had parental consent. The marriage records show the names of the bride and groom; occupations of both parties; whether single, widow(er)ed or divorced; ages of both parties; names and addressed of witnesses; names of parents of both parties, including the maiden name of mothers; name and denomination of the minister. In 1855 alone the records also identified whether either party had been married before, if so, how many children had been produced, and how many of these were still alive. Also, the date and place of birth of the bride and groom were given, and whether these births had been registered.

Death records

Death records show the name; date, time and place of death; cause of death and the name of the Doctor if present; occupation; marital status; gender, age; place of death; usual residence, if not the same as the place of death; whether married or widowed; parents' names, including mother's maiden name, and whether the parents were alive or dead; occupation of father; informant's name and sometime address. In 1855 and from 1861 onwards you will also find details of the spouse. In 1855 only you will also find details of where the deceased was born and how long they and lived in the place where they died and the names and ages of children the deceased.

Because the certificates are available at the NAS on a self-service basis, research in them can proceed very quickly, often back four or more generations in a single visit. You will usually find that each certificate comes on a microfiche card, a small plastic sheet containing photographic copies of dozens of certificates. This protects the original certificate from wear and tear, and can be easily read using one of the microfiche machines in the search room.

1855 is usually the cut-off point, although death certificates can extend the tree well before this date. For instance, if someone who was born in 1790 lived until the grand old age of seventy-five, their death certificate (circa 1865) would give two more names to add to the top of the tree, taking things back to a couple born around 1770 or earlier.

Many early Scottish civil registration certificates can be consulted on microform in LDS family history centres around the world. The IGI (International Genealogical Index) has good coverage of births and marriages from Scottish civil registration records for the years 1855–1875 and it can therefore be a useful tool for tracing events then.

GROS indexes and images of the records are online at ScotlandsPeople www.scotlandspeople.gov.uk. The statutory births index contains entries from the indexes to the civil registers of births for all Scotland, from 1855 until 2006. Images of statutory births from 1855 to 1908 are available to view on this site. A digital image is a scan of the microfiche copy of the original register page containing the entry in which you are interested.

The statutory marriages index contains entries from the paper indexes to the civil registers of marriages for all Scotland, from 1855 until 1933 and images taken from the original registers covering the same period.

The statutory deaths index contains entries from the paper indexes to the civil registers of deaths for all Scotland, from 1855 until 2006. Images of Statutory deaths from 1855 to 1958 are available to view on this site.

The ScotlandsPeople website also provides details of the registration district's county and the GROS's official list at www.gro-scoland.gov.uk/famrec/hlpsrch/list-of-parishes-registration-districts.html. This provides the county or burgh in which the registration district lies, and its start date. It is also easy to look them up on www.maps.google.co.uk/.

After 1753, when English law forbad irregular marriages, a number of people who objected to marrying in a church were married in border centres where the couple's own consent to marriage before witnesses was legal under Scottish Law. Gretna is the most famous of these. Marriages were conducted by self appointed ministers at the border Toll booths along the few roads into Scotland. A searchable database of 4,500 marriages from 1795 to

1895 is provided by Achievements Ltd. at http://www.achievements.co.uk/services/gretna/index.php.

Wills and Testamentary Records

Once the date of an ancestor has been discovered, it is worth finding out whether they left a will. One should not assume that because the family was poor members would not have made a will. Sometimes those who made a will were determined that their money or possessions went to the right person when they died. Strangely it doesn't always follow that people who were in comfortable positions left wills. People from well-to-do families sometimes disposed of their wealth before they died in order to avoid death duties.

Although Scots law can often be radically different to its neighbour south of the border in terms of wills it worked in quite similar fashion. Wills and testaments provide useful details of what people owned, and to whom they were related. The people generally identified in these records are spouses and children, but you may also find details of parents, brothers, sisters, nieces and nephews and grandchildren and so on.

In Scotland there were also services to heirs (called retours). These concerned the inheritance of land held direct from the Crown, and also cases of complicated inheritance, such as grandchildren inheriting from their grandparents because their parents were dead. Retours were also used to appoint 'tutors' or guardians for fatherless children ('pupils').

The Will

A will is a document stating how the individual wants to dispose of their property after his death. The executor of his estate, who is confirmed by a testament approved by the courts, will carry out those wishes.

The property fell into two categories under Scottish law. Buildings, anything to do with land and mineral rights, known as heritable property, went to the eldest son (the law of primogeniture). The rest, called movable property, consisted of goods, money, and other items. Traditionally this was divided into thirds. The widow received a third (*jus relictae*), another third was divided equally among the children (*legitim*), with the remainders, the deid's part, consisting of bequests by the deceased. In the absence of either widow or children, movable property would be divided into two parts, or simply became all the deid part, although that always had to be confirmed by the court.

Testaments

Testaments fell into a further two categories, known as testament testamentars and testament datives. The former came into effect when the dead person left a will, and had an introduction, an inventory of possessions of the dead person, the will itself (or a copy), and a confirmation clause. Testament datives only applied when no will was left, and were essentially the same as a testament testamentary, except for the will itself. Until the beginning of the 19th century, testaments tended to relate only to movable property, but things quickly altered to cover all property.

Finding Wills

Until 1824, the Commissary Courts recorded testaments within their own boundaries. The Phillimore Atlas and Index (Phillimore, 2003) will show you which court had jurisdiction over your ancestors' home parishes, and more detail is given in J Gibson and E Churchill's *Probate Jurisdictions: Where to Look for Wills* (FFHS, 2002).

From that point, however, that changed to being a function of the Sheriff Courts. Most of these records are in the NAS indexed, 1824–75 with annual indexes thereafter to 1959, called calandars of confirmations and inventories.

www.scotlandspeople.gov.uk is the best database for researching wills and testaments, with an index of more than 600,000 going from the 1513 to the early 20th century. Even an index entry is valuable, offering not only the name of the deceased, but their occupation and where they lived, along with where and when the testament was recorded. Be aware, however, that an index entry won't give you the date of death or what the estate was worth – you'll need a copy of the will itself for that, and you can find images of wills from this period which are available for a fee.

Land Records

Estate records held by the National Archives of Scotland are an invaluable source for life in the Scottish countryside. Those who rented and worked the land are mainly to be found in the rentals (rent rolls) of estates, and the records of leases, known as tacks, and in miscellaneous records kept by the factor, the proprietor's estate manager and agent.

The most important classes of records are:

Rentals (rent rolls)

Rentals can often simply consist of summary accounts of the annual income of the estate without mentioning individuals. More helpful are those which contain information such as the names of the tenants, the name, acreage and value of the land leased, the year in which the lease began, its duration, and payments made in cash, kind or labour. Sometimes there are also notes on the buildings leased and remarks about the tenant's behaviour or character by the estate factor. Where individuals are mentioned, rentals only give the name of the head of the house and do not list wives, children or other dependants.

Leases (tacks)

Leases may provide more information than rentals, and they are often catalogued as a separate series. Also worth exploring if possible is the factor's correspondence, which usually contains at least some letters from (or about) prospective tenants. Correspondence with existing tenants often concerns requests for the reduction of rent, and a myriad of other grievances that throw light on their personal circumstances.

Household accounts

As servants were not the factor's responsibility, correspondence concerning individual maids and footmen is much less common, and usually survives only in family letters. Household accounts can sometimes provide evidence of their names and occupations.

Locating Records

Locating surviving records for a particular locality is largely a matter of finding out the name of the landowner of the day and then checking the indexes and catalogues in different archives to see if any of his records survive. You may already know the name of the local landowner, in which case you should consult the National Register of Archives maintained by The National Archives: Historical Manuscripts Commission (TNA) and the Scottish Archive Network (SCAN) online catalogue http://www.nationalarchives.gov.uk/nra/default.asp

It may also be relevant to consult the National Archives of Scotland (NAS) electronic catalogue at http://www.nas.gov.uk/catalogues/default.asp (most of the estate records in the NAS are part of the Gifts and Deposits (NAS ref. GD) series).

If you do not know the identity of the landowner(s) in a particular area, there are several publications which can aid you. These publications, as well as others, should be available through a good library, as well as being available for consultation at the NAS:

Ordnance Survey Gazetteer, 6 vols., by Francis H. Groome (Edinburgh, 1883). *Statistical Account of Scotland*, 3 Series, numerous volumes compiled by the ministers of the Church of Scotland, various editors (Edinburgh, 1791–1799, 1845 and 1987). Also available online at Edinburgh University's EDINA website.
A Directory of Landownership in Scotland c 1770, edited by Loretta R Timperley, Scottish Record Society, (Edinburgh, 1976).

The following list is a guide to the major estate collections held by the NAS:

NAS reference	Family	Dates
GD25	Marquess of Ailsa	1290–1940
GD16	Earls of Airlie	1161–1954
GD433	Earl of Balfour	1839–1954
GD112	Earls of Breadalbane	1306–1914
GD224	Dukes of Buccleuch	1165–1947
GD18	Clerk of Penicuik	1373–1966
GD305	Earls of Cromartie	1257–1960
GD45	Earls of Dalhousie	1127–1965
GD446	Douglas of Strathendry	1477–1883
GD233	Earls of Dundonald	1585–1993
GD3	Earls of Eglinton	1363–1931
GD406	Dukes of Hamilton	1543–1858
GD26	Earls of Leven and Melville	1200–1853
GD40	Marquesses of Lothian	1140–1987
GD201	Macdonald of Clanranald	1531–1864
GD124	Earls of Morton	1250–1940
GD51	Viscounts of Melville	1343–1940
GD150	Earls of Morton	1250–1940
GD220	Dukes of Montrose	1175–1941
GD160	Earls of Perth	1197–1880
GD44	Dukes of Richmond and Gordon	1357–1903
GD248	Earls of Seafield	1215–1939

GD135	Earls of Stair	1358–1955
GD193	Steel Maitland of Sauchie	1489–1954
GD46	Stewart-Mackenzie of Seaforth	1467–1939
GD28	Marquess of Tweeddale	1166–1792

All land in Scotland was held from the Crown by grants known as feus, which could in turn by sublet by grant. Land could not be bequeathed by will as in England, Wales and Ireland, but passed directly to the next living heir who, in the case of those hold land from the Crown, had to prove their right at a Sherriff's inquest. The resulting decisions, or retours, recorded in Latin until 1847, survive from about 1530 and are at the NAS. These are indexed and abstracts of the records to 1699 are also in print.

Register of Sasines

The word "sasine", which shares the same root as the English word "seize", refers in Scots law to the transfer of what is known as 'heritable property' primarily land and buildings, but also other, geographically fixed, items such as mineral rights (fundamentally important in parts of Scotland from the 18th century onwards) and fishing rights.

In Scots' law the sale of land was conducted before witnesses and recorded in notaries' protocol books which are now held at the NAS and the regional record officers. Many have been published by record societies and are listed in D. and W.B. Stevenson's *Scottish Texts & Calendars, An Analytical Guide to Serial Publications* (Royal Historical Society, London and Scottish Royal Historical Society, Edinburgh, 1987). It will normally detail the names of the new and previous owners and will give a basic description of the property transferred. There will usually be an indication of the price paid for the property.

There were several attempts to start a national register of sasines in Scotland. One early attempt, The Secretary's Register, started in 1599 and ended in 1609 so it is very incomplete. Its records are now incorporated into the two registers that succeeded it, from 1617, known as the General and Particular Registers of Sasines.

The Particular Registers was divided into counties which covered all of Scotland, except the three Lothian counties. They are indexed up to 1780 except for the counties of Orkney and Shetland, Perth, Renfrew and Glasgow, Roxburgh, Selkirk and Peebles, Stirling and Clackmannan and

Wigtown. Particular Registers that have not been indexed are best searched using the minute books or, failing these, searching through the register itself.

The general register was also used to record details of properties that were spread over more than one county. It is indexed to 1735. The period 1736–80 can be searched using the minute books in NAS RH62.

From 1781 onwards, there are printed abridgements of sasines, covering the Particular and General Registers (the latter was abandoned in 1868). These have now been digitized and are fully indexed up to the present by place (except between 1831 and 1871) and person. Some registers of sasines have also been microfilmed by the Mormons.

From 1681 there was also separate registers for about seventy Royal Burghs. With the exception of the Glasgow burgh register, and the Aberdeen and Dundee pre-1809 registers (which are held in the respective city archives) these records are held in the National Archives of Scotland (NAS) under the catalogue reference B.

The publication by the Stair Society of *A Formulary of Old Scots Documents* (edited by P.Gouldesbrough, 1985) contains, among many other useful examples, the complete transcript of a Latin instrument of sasine with translation.

Scottish Land Registry

The Land Register is a map-based system (unlike the Register of Sasines) which contains a property description tied to the Ordnance Map by a title plan, ownership details and conditions which affect the property. The Land Register is gradually taking over from the Register of Sasines and is now operational throughout the whole of Scotland.

The Scottish Land Registry is at the Registers of Scotland Excutive Agency for details see http://www.ros.gov.uk/index.html

Valuation Rolls

Provision for a uniform system of valuation throughout Scotland was made by the Lands Valuation (Scotland) Act of 1854, to commence in 1855, covering all lands and heritages in Scotland including railways and canals. These name the proprietor, the tenant and the occupier separately, thought those paying a yearly rent of less than £4 were not included. Unlike a census return they do not list any other residents in a property. On the other hand they may provide more information on the family during the ten years between censuses.

The Valuation Rolls are arranged by counties and burghs, some of the burghs being merged with their counties in 1929 and 1956. Some rolls, particularly for the more populous areas such as Aberdeen, Dundee, Edinburgh and Glasgow, can be awkward to search. For these areas there will often be several volumes covering each year. Unfortunately most valuation rolls are not indexed and an often time-consuming search through the volumes in question will be required before you find the entry for the property concerned. The NAS holds copies of all valuation rolls until 1989 (ref VR) when the Community Charge ('Poll Tax') for domestic ratepayers was introduced and replaced the previous system. Local archives and libraries often hold valuation rolls for their particular district.

Registers of Deeds

Deeds are a major source of Scottish genealogical information which include information on land transactions, marriage settlements, disposal of property after death and leases of land to name but a few. Deeds will show names and designations of family members, particularly in marriage contracts, they may indicate the sort of business people were involved in (e.g. co-partnery agreements) and may also indicate the movement of heritable property (land, buildings) in some cases.

A deed is a legal agreement, obligation or other document registered with a court in order to establish the basis of a legal right before proceeding to a related legal action. In registering the deed, the person presenting it paid a fee to a court clerk who copied the document into the register and then kept the original document. This original document was called the warrant. While for most genealogical purposes the recorded version is satisfactory, the warrant will show the signatures of the parties to the deed.

In copying the document, many clerks also made a brief note of the entry in a separate minute book. These were kept to prove that they had done their work but they were also used as an index if records had to be retrieved. Modern searchers can use them in the same way. Once registered, the parties received certified extracts of the document.

Location of Deeds

Deeds could be registered in a number of places: in the Register of Deeds at the Court of Session, in sheriff courts, in royal burghs, in commissary courts or in the courts of the heritable jurisdictions (the private courts of major landowners). The heritable jurisdictions were abolished in 1748 and the registers of deeds in commissary courts were abolished in 1809. If you do not know where a deed was recorded, searching can be a bit of a guessing game. The more important the deed, the more likely it is to be registered in the Register of Deeds of the Court of Session. Otherwise a deed about a relatively minor matter of local interest could involve you in a trawl of the deeds registers maintained by various other courts.

The Register of Deeds of the Court of Session

The formal title for the Register of Deeds is the Books of Council and Session. The series commenced in 1554 and was based at Edinburgh. It is now held in the National Archives of Scotland (NAS ref. RD). The register contains official copies of deeds presented to the Court of Session, the highest civil court in Scotland. The full range of deeds was recorded there. There are contracts or other obligations such as sales of contracts, dispositions of heritable property, marriage settlements, bonds, shipping agreements, building contracts and occasionally some apprenticeship agreements. While the register does contain a very few title deeds, it does not contain a systematic record of landownership. Title deeds are normally to be found in the Register of Sasines. Unlike the Register of Sasines, the Register of Deeds is a voluntary register. By registering a deed at the Court of Session, the undertaking then had the force of a decree of court.

In the register of deeds you can find many sorts of documents that may be of use to family historians.

There are indexes in the NSA for the Register of Deeds of the Court of Session for the years 1554–1595, 1661–1702, 1705–7, 1714–15, 1750–2, 1765, and from 1770 to the present. For the gap periods where there is no index, there are usually minute books that can act as a substitute.

Sheriff Court Registers of Deeds

Not all the sheriff courts kept a register of deeds, but there is at least one for each county. These records are kept in the National Archives of Scotland (NAS ref. SC). The registers of deeds for the sheriff courts vary in their covering dates from court to court and not all survive. The earliest surviving register is for Perth Sheriff Court, from 1570. From 1809, the registers were kept quite consistently. A few of the sheriff courts have indexes for their deeds registers after 1809 but the majority do not. Consequently searching them can be laborious, involving the use of minute books, or sometimes simply leafing through the pages.

Royal Burgh Registers of Deeds
There are registers of deeds for almost half of the 66 royal burghs. These are held in the National Archives of Scotland (NAS ref. B). The dates for these registers vary considerably (the earliest being that for Edinburgh in 1561) and they extend into the 20th century. Unfortunately, only some of the registers are indexed.

Commissary Court Registers of Deeds
Before 1809, the commissary courts could register deeds as well. These records are held in the National Archives of Scotland (NAS ref. CC). Apart from Peebles, 1755–62 (NAS ref. CC18), the commissary court deeds are not indexed, so that searching them can be time consuming unless you have a very strong lead as to when a document was registered.

Local Court Registers of Deeds
Some local courts also kept registers of deeds, before 1748. Where these survive, they are usually in the National Archives of Scotland (NAS ref. RH11). Some of the gaps in the registers are filled by the information given in other court books. There should be a note within the relevant catalogue to local court records should this be the case. The local court registers of deeds are not indexed, so that searching them can be time consuming unless you have a very strong lead as to when a document was registered.

Church Records

The Old Parish Records
Civil registration in Scotland dates from 1855. Before that date, the registration of baptisms, marriages and burials was the responsibility of the Scottish church. This information was recorded in the old parish registers (OPRs). Although parishes were ordered to keep registers in 1551, records were often only kept sporadically. The earlier Scottish register is for the parish of Errol in Perthshire in which the first entry is dated 1553.

It is important to remember that many births and baptisms, proclamations and marriages and burials were not recorded for a variety of reasons. In some cases parents were unwilling to pay to have their children baptised. In other cases the minister or clerk forgot to record an event; registers being incomplete or damaged for periods; families may have fallen out with the minister; or people were members of other religious denominations (e.g. Roman Catholics, Free Church, Episcopalians etc.)

To trace an individual in the OPRs, it helps to have some idea of where that person lived. Census returns can be very useful in identifying birthplaces of those alive after 1841.

The information contained in the OPRs can vary immensely. For the birth of a child you will usually be given the names of both parents (including maiden name of mother) and often an address and names of witnesses (often relatives).

A marriage will sometimes name relatives of the couple. Burial registers usually provide the least information, if they exist at all for the period you need. Evidence of deaths comes from the kirk session records showing payments made for digging the grave or hiring the parish mortcloth (a black cloth draped over the coffin).

Regular marriages were preceded by the proclamation of banns in the parish churches of both parties, with at least two witnesses present. Proclamations were supposed to be made on three consecutive Sundays in order to make public the couple's intention to marry. These proclamations were entered in the OPR. Session clerks seldom bothered recording the date of the wedding itself: if only one date is given this will usually be that of the proclamation. The wedding generally took place within six weeks of the proclamation. The OPR will include the names of the parties and the date of the proclamation. They may also include the parishes of residence, marriage date and the names of witnesses.

Marriages not carried out the Church of Scotland ministers, or marriages created by people living together without any formal ceremony were known as irregular marriages. Until 1834, despite such unions being illegal, the kirk sessions often summoned wrong-doers and fined them before acknowledging the marriage: the union may appear in the OPRs, possibly identified as 'irregular'. Some irregular marriages were investigated in the law courts, and may turn up in their records.

After 1855, if a couple who had married irregularly wanted legal recognition of their union, they might approach a sheriff court and obtain a warrant for the marriage to be recorded by the local registrar, and this will be noted on the GROS record.

Church of Scotland

The church collections form a significant proportion of the holdings of the National Archives of Scotland (NAS). The material dates from the 16th century onwards and includes a small number of records from the pre-Reformation era. Original church records in the NAS are referenced CH. The records of the parish kirk sessions, presbyteries and synods of the post-Reformation Church of Scotland are referenced CH.2. You can look up the name of your parish in the index to the CH.2. repertory to get an exact reference number for the parish kirk.

Some kirk session and other church records have been moved to local archives. Microfilms of most of these records up to 1860 are however available in the NAS. The CH repertory will tell you if the records you want are on microfilm.

The NSA does not hold records for baptisms, marriages and deaths, which the minister compiled until 1855. These Old Parish Registers are kept, along with the later statutory registers, by the Registrar-General of Scotland and may be consulted on microfilm, on payment of a fee, in New Register House.

Ministers of the Church of Scotland

Fasti Ecclesiae Scoticanae is a list of the ministers of the Church of Scotland (published in ten volumes) which is based on the records of Kirk sessions, Synods and General Assemblies. The entries are arranged by Synod, then Presbytery, then Parish. The details of a minister's career (and other biographical information about him and sometimes his family) are given under his last incumbency. However, each entry gives details of any parish to which a minister transferred so that you can easily trace a minister's career through to the final, detailed entry.

Episcopalian Records

In 1690, 500 clergy formed the Episcopal Church of Scotland. It only retained any real footing in the north-east, and many of its early registers have been lost, or remain in private hands. The NAS has some records (CH.12) and microfilms of some registers in class RH.4/179–185 and appendices 51–7. For others, look in the NRA. For ministers see D M Bertie's *Scottish Episcopal Clergy 1689–2000* (Edinburgh, 2000).

Cameronians

In the 1680s many Covenanters followed the preacher Richard Cameron, and became Cameronians, and in 1743, Reformed Presbyterians. In 1876, most were united with the Free Church of Scotland, and thus most records, such as they are, are in NAS class CH. A few congregations remained independent and retain their own records.

The Secession Churches

Since 1690, the Church of Scotland has seen several substantial secessions. One such group led by Ebenezer Erskine left in 1733 to form the Associate Presbytery. This in turn split into the Burghers and Anti-Burghers, each of which formed 'Auld Licht' and 'New Licht' factions. In 1760, the Relief Presbytery split from the Church of Scotland, later absorbing the Associate Presbytery's New Licht groups.

The Free Church of Scotland broke from the Church of Scotland in the Disruption of 1843. The Free Church spread rapidly, and by 1851 had 880 chapels. In 1893 yet another session created the Free Presbyterian Church of Scotland

In 1847 the United Presbyterian Church of Scotland was created by unifying the United Session Church and the Relief Church. In 1900 it merged with parts of the Free Church having also absorbed the Associate Synod, Burghers and Anti-Burghers and Reformed Presbyterian Kirk. In 1929, this in turn merged back into the Church of Scotland.

If you family does not appear in the OPR it is because they had become nonconformists. After 1855 you can tell which denomination by seeing where they married, or look in Groome's Gazetter or the *Statistical Accounts* to see what nonconformist chapel was nearest your ancestors' home.

As the United Presbyterian Church's registers include many records of its earlier constituent parts, it's worth searching its collection in CH3 first. Some surviving registers are in local archives (sometimes with microfilm copies in NAS).

Methodists

John Wesley's first visit to Scotland was in April 1751 when he made a two day visit to Musselburgh in East Lothian. Wesley in all was to make twenty-two visits to Scotland between then and 1790. Sir Walter Scott writing almost forty years after the event, described hearing Wesley preach: 'When I was about 12 years old I heard Wesley preach...standing on a chair in Kelso churchyard. He was a venerable figure... and told many excellent stories'. According to Wesley's own *Journal* this event took place on the evening of Friday 14 June 1782, and was three days short of his 79th birthday. He writes: 'I spoke strong words in the evening, concerning judgement to come: and some seemed to awake out of sleep'. At the time of Wesley's death there were only eight Methodist 'Chapels' opened in Scotland. Throughout the nineteenth and early twentieth centuries Methodist societies emerged in various places; some prospered, some survived, and some disappeared. Always strongest in the west of Scotland's industrial heart, and from Edinburgh up the east coast, it reached its peak in numbers in the late 1950s at about 13,500 members (although this number did not include the remaining *societies* in Berwickshire and Dumfries which were administered by English Districts; or indeed Shetland). Methodism in Scotland however was never to achieve the proportional numerical relationship to the Church of Scotland as it did to the Church of England in the south.

Early Methodists appear in the OPR, but later congregations started keeping their own registers. Generally records of rural churches went to university archives, records of city churches went to local authority archives and at the NAS (CH.11).

Quakers

The Religious Society of Friends, also known as 'Quakers' or 'Friends', originated in the north-west of England during the mid-seventeenth century. Until 1786, there were two Yearly Meetings, at Aberdeen & Edinburgh, within which various Monthly and other subordinate Meetings existed at various times. In 1786, they were replaced by North Britain Half Years Meeting, subordinate to London Yearly Meeting. This was renamed Scotland General Meeting in 1807.

From the beginning the Quakers were among the best record-keepers. Monthly meetings contain registers of birth, marriages and deaths, minutes of meetings, accounts of sufferings and charity papers. As a result Quaker records contain a great deal of information about local affairs. Most of these very detailed records are at the NAS in CH10, including a list of all Scottish Quaker births, deaths and marriages up to 1890.

Roman Catholic Church Records

The NAS holds photocopies of Roman Catholic registers of baptisms, marriages, deaths and communicants (RH.21).

Scottish Catholic Archives at Columba House, Edinburgh holds some church records and has information about others. Most dioceses have deposited their historical records at Columba House, and retain only current records. There is also a great deal of material from Scots Catholic Colleges overseas at Columba House. The Archdiocese of Glasgow and Diocese of Paisley retain their historic records.

The archdiocesan archive holds, in the Curial Offices at 196 Clyde Street, Glasgow, G1 4JY, original registers with a starting-date prior to the introduction of civil registration in Scotland in 1855. It is possible, by prior appointment, for enquirers to visit the archive and search the registers. Appointments should be made by contacting the archivist either by letter, or by telephone on 0141 226 5898 x154.

Jewish Records
Founded in 1987 and based in Garnethill Synagogue in Glasgow (Scotland's oldest), the Scottish Jewish Archives Centre aims to document and illustrate the religious, organisational, social, economic, political, cultural and family life of Jews in Scotland since the eighteenth century. The Centre collects a wide range of material, and its large collection includes old synagogue minute books and registers, membership lists, over 6,000 photographs, oral history recordings, annual reports of many communal organisations, a small library of books of Scottish Jewish interest, friendly society regalia, personal papers, war medals, ceremonial keys, newspapers, magazines, trophies, plaques, paintings and sculptures.

Poor Law Records

Before 1845 when poor relief became the responsibility of parochial boards set up for the purpose, the amelioration of poverty was in the hands of the church, which meant a mix of the kirk session and the heritors (who were responsible for the church building itself, but whose responsibilities often extended further).

Scottish Poor Relief Records from Before 1845
Kirk session records and poor rolls are the main sources for finding names of those receiving poor relief before 1845. Although parishes were free to levy a poor rate, less than 20% did, relying on other income to take care of the poor within their parish.

It's possible to find kirk session records dating back to the 1600s, but from the 1700s onwards, many more still exist (the same is true for heritors' minutes). The place to begin looking is in the National Archives of Scotland. Many are in the possession of local archives or even the kirk itself.

Scottish Parochial Board Records After 1845

Following the establishment of the 1845 Poor Law (Scotland) Act, parochial boards were set up to deal with poor relief (these became the forerunners of parish councils). Some paupers qualified for weekly handouts of money, called "outdoor relief," but the majority entered the poorhouse – often boards would come together to build poorhouses for paupers from several parishes. It was only after 1921 that the unemployed became eligible for poor relief.

Each parish kept its own general poor register, listing all those who received relief of any kind. The NAS holds parochial board records for some parishes in East Lothian (NAS ref. CO7/7, DC5/4–5 and DC7/4), Midlothian (NAS ref. CO2/77–91) and Wigtownshire (NAS ref. CO4/30–47). For information on records for all other areas of Scotland you should contact the relevant local archive.

Each parish had a poor roll, revised annually and available for public inspection. The registers of poor, normally bound volumes of printed forms, contained the basic information about applicants admitted to the poor roll in this way. For each pauper the register gives the name, address, marital status, age, birthplace, occupation, whether disabled and if so how, financial circumstances, and a record of the decision by the parochial board.

If the register hasn't survived in a parish it might still be worthwhile investigating the minutes of the parochial board. The records of the parochial boards can sometimes be found in the heritors' records, but more frequently they are found in the county, district and burgh records. Each parochial board had to keep a roll of the poor to whom it gave relief and these can contain a considerable amount of detail about each pauper – name, age, country and place of birth, marital status and details of spouse and children. The records may also include applications for those who were not successful in receiving relief.

School Records

The Scots have always been justifiably proud of an education system which established a breath-taking array of parish schools, burgh schools, grammar schools and adventure schools in nearly every parish. It is important to note that, although a wide variety of records relating to schools is available, few of these will contain information on pupils.

Surviving records of burgh schools are normally with other burgh records, held either by the local archive office, or the NAS. However, it is unusual for specific education records to survive: most references to burgh schools and schoolmasters especially the appointment of Burgh Schoolmasters lie within the general series of council minutes, which are often un-indexed, and it may take some searching to identify relevant references. The Scottish Burgh Record Society has published extracts from the records of Aberdeen, Edinburgh, Glasgow, Peebles, Stirling, Lanark and Paisley and these are fully indexed.

Heritors were the landed proprietors of the parish, and were formerly liable for the payment of public burdens connected with the parish, including the provision of schools in the parish. Surviving heritors' records for the whole of Scotland (NAS ref. HR) are held by NAS. These may include references to the provision of a school, schoolmaster and schoolhouse within the general heritors' minutes. Records of individual kirk sessions (NAS ref. CH2 and CH3) are also worth searching: for example Kinghorn Kirk Session records include a volume of minutes of the Committee of St Andrews' School 1835–39 (NAS ref. CH2/472/16). References to schools may also be found scattered through the general kirk session, presbytery, or synod records.

The Education (Scotland) Act of 1872 opened formal education to all children, and placed local control and funding of schools in the hands of school boards. Surviving records of school boards are usually held by the archive office of the creating authority. NAS holds the surviving county council records for Aberdeenshire, Dumfriesshire, East Lothian, Fife, Inverness-shire, Midlothian, Peeblesshire, Selkirkshire, Sutherland and Wigtownshire (NAS ref. CO). There is an extensive set of minutes of various school boards in the records of East Lothian county council (eg Borthwick School Board, NAS ref. CO2/105/1).

Current records of individual schools remain with the schools, but older records of local authority schools are often held on deposit by local archives. These mainly comprise schools' admission registers and headmasters' log books.

School inspection reports
Growth in school numbers led to the appointment in 1840 of the first of Her Majesty's Inspectors of Schools, and the series of HMI reports in NAS is one of the best sources of information on individual schools. The main series of school Inspection reports are (NAS ref. ED16, 17 and 18). Sometimes personal details about specific teachers are included such as their age, period of service, qualifications and former employment. Reports on independent and grant-maintained schools are also found in NAS ref. ED32, where a number of kindergarten and nursery schools, such as Kinloss RAF Nursery School (NAS ref. ED32/81), appear alongside Scotland's major public schools such as Loretto (NAS ref. ED32/302) and Gordonstoun (NAS ref. ED32/310).

Examination results
Results of the Leaving, Senior Leaving and Scottish Leaving Certificate Examination Registers, 1908–1965 (NAS ref. ED36) and Results of Senior Leaving Certificate Examination Results during the war years, 1940–1945 (NAS ref. ED40) are held by the NAS.

Educational organisations and endowed institutions
Some gifted and deposited collections are of particular interest to education researchers. The Dick Bequest, whose records begin in 1727 and end in 1990, provided grants to augment the salaries of schoolmasters in the north east of Scotland (NAS ref. GD1/4). The registers are a useful source of information on the careers of individual teachers, as are the records of the Scottish Society for the Propagation of Christian Knowledge (SSPCK) , founded 1707 (NAS ref. GD95). Teachers also feature in the records of the Educational Institute of Scotland (NAS ref. GD342). Records of this organisation begin in 1785, so it is, with the SSPCK and Dick Bequest records, a good early source on the lives of teachers. These records deal with individual schools and schoolmasters, though not pupils. Records of individual schools include Edinburgh's John Watson's (NAS ref. GD352), Dean Orphanage (NAS ref. GD417) and George Heriot's (NAS ref. GD421) schools.
A number of well-known Scottish public and grammar schools have published their registers. These include *Aberdeen Grammar School, 1795–1919*, annotated from 1863 by T Wall (1923); *Edinburgh Academy, from its foundation in 1824*, (1914); *Fettes College, 1870 to 1909* (1909); *Loretto School, 1825–1925* (1927); *Melville College* (Edinburgh Institution*), 1832–1932* (1933); *Merchiston Castle School, 1833–1962* (1962); *St Leonard's School, St Andrews*, (for girls), I

1877–1895, ii 1895–1900 (1895 and 1901); *The Glenalmond Register 1950–1985 and Supplement 1900–1949*, published by Hunter & Foulis Ltd, 1986.

For lists of schoolmasters check David Dobson's, *Scottish schoolmasters of the 17th century* (St Andrews, 1995) and *SSPCK Schoolmasters, 1709–1872* edited by A S Cowper and published by the Scottish Record Society (1997).

Military Records

Scottish soldiers 1603 to 1707

The main NAS record of individuals in the Scottish army before 1707 is the series of muster rolls (NAS ref. E100). These are arranged by regiment and companies or troops. Most are dated after 1680, although the earliest dates from 1641. They name all the officers and men in a troop or company at a certain place and date. Ranks are also stated, other than for troopers.

Without knowing which regiment your ancestor served in, however, any search through the muster rolls will prove to be an arduous and time-consuming task. Of some assistance may be the fact that many regimental recruits came from the estate owned by the colonel or his family. Therefore, if you know the estate or even area where your ancestor lived, and can match this to a likely regiment, a search through the muster rolls may prove to be less problematic. Some of these rolls are also printed in C Dalton's *The Scots Army, 1661–1688* (republished in 1989 by Greenhill Books) although only officers appear in his index. Private family papers in the NAS or other archives may also provide details of individuals who had been granted a commission to be a colonel of a regiment.

If your ancestor was an officer then the chances of finding a record of him are better. Commissions in the army were granted by the Crown and from 1670 some were recorded in the warrant books of the Secretary for Scotland. A sift through the state papers series of records (NAS ref. SP4) covering the relevant dates might be worth while. The volumes are indexed or at least contain a contents page. The commissions supply only the name, rank, company and regiment of the officer and give no other personal details. The SP4 commissions are indexed in Dalton's *The Scots Army, 1661–1688* and also in his book *English Army Lists and Commission Registers, 1661–1714*. Finally, there is also a small series of commissions from 1643 and 1689–1827 in a miscellaneous series of records (NAS ref. RH9/9). Again, commissions can occasionally be found in private family collections and so a trawl through the NAS military source list might be worthwhile.

Militia records

The only large group of post-Union military records held by the NAS are those for the militia and, more recently, the territorial army. As conscription was by ballot, only some men were actually made to serve. These run mostly from the late eighteenth to the mid-nineteenth centuries, but are concentrated around the Napoleonic War period (1800 -1815). The Army regarded the militia as a source of recruits for the Line Regiments; it is said that the British Army at Waterloo presented a sight which was anything but uniform, so many men in the ranks were still wearing the tunics of their former militia regiments.

The principal militia material in the NAS is to be found in the catalogues for the sheriff courts or county councils. The relevant records, if they survive, will be catalogued under the lieutenancy/militia or miscellaneous sections, which generally appear at the end of each catalogue.

Many militia records may also be found in private collections in the NAS, usually in the papers of the local landowners responsible for compiling lists of men able to bear arms in a particular area.

A militiaman's family could be eligible for assistance and claims for this money can sometimes be found in the militia records noted above. There is a record of government payments to the wives and children of militiamen in and around the Edinburgh area for the period 1803 -1815. This is in the NAS Exchequer records series (NAS ref. E327/147–158).

Records relating to volunteer and territorial forces, nineteenth to twentieth centuries, can be found among the Ministry of Defence files (NAS ref. MD).

Local archives in Scotland may also have militia records, perhaps as part of the records of former county councils. You can find listings of local archives on the SCAN website and on the ARCHON section of TNA's website.

Scottish soldiers in the British army after 1707

After 1707 the army was controlled from London and most British army records are held at The National Archives, London (TNA). Their website has a comprehensive section on military records. The National Archives, London, has records for men and women who left the services before the end of 1920. It is important that you know when your ancestor was in the forces and the regiment or unit with which he served. It was customary before the First World War for regiments to recruit primarily within a local district, but of course many Scotsmen joined English regiments.

Officers can be found in published *Army Lists, Navy Lists* and *Air Force Lists*. From 1740, all officers were listed in the published *Army List* which appeared at least annually. *Hart's Army List* was published between 1839 and 1915. Both series are available at Kew and at major Scottish archives and libraries.

For the nineteenth century The National Archives, London, has several series of records detailing the service of officers and an alphabetical card index to these records is available. TNA has correspondence about the sale and purchase of commissions between 1793 and 1871 in series WO 31. This contains a great deal of valuable genealogical information. For officers commissioned before 1754 try the Commission books in WO25/1. Manuscript lists of army officers are kept from 1702 to 1752 (WO64).

For information on ancestors who served in the rank and file between 1760 and 1913 the most useful records available at The National Archives, London, are the soldiers' documents in series WO 97. Soldiers' documents up to 1854 have been indexed by surname and this index is available in the Microfilm Reading Room at Kew.

The majority of the army service records for the period between 1914 and the end of 1920 were destroyed in the Second World War. Those documents that survived are in series WO 363. There is also a series of service records, in WO 364, for men who received a pension after the First World War.

Officers and men also appear on campaign medal rolls, which before 1913 are in WO 100. During the First World War almost all men who served in the Army were entitled to at least two campaign medals. The medal record cards at the PRO will tell you which regiments(s) a man served with, which medals he was entitled to, and approximately when and where he served.

Other Scottish soldiers and sailors had their pensions paid by the Royal Chelsea Hospital or by Greenwich Hospital. Records of these pensions, 1842–1862 and 1882–1883, are in WO22/141–205 and WO 22/209–225. They can be used to trace changes of residence and dates of death.

Remember that many Scottish regiments have their own museums and these will often have collections of information about past units and the men who served in them. You may also want to contact the National War Museum at Edinburgh Castle. The museum has a copy of the published Army Lists, a microfiche index to the roll of service medals for the First World War, and a small collection of regimental casualty lists.

The General Register Office for Scotland also holds the following armed forces records: the Army Returns (births, deaths and marriages of Scots at military stations abroad from 1881–1959); Service Departments Registers (births, deaths and marriages from 1959 outside the UK relating to Scots serving in or employed by HM Forces); and marriages by Army chaplains outside the UK since 1892. The War registers also record deaths of: Scottish soldiers during the South African War (1899–1902); Scots serving as Warrant Officers, Non-Commissioned Officers or Men in the Army (but not officers) and also Petty Officers or Men in the Royal Navy during World War I (1914–1918), and Scots in the Armed Forces during World War II (1939–1945).

The Commonwealth War Graves Commission website http://www.cwgc. org/ has a searchable database covering service personnel who died in the First and Second World Wars.

The Veterans Agency website http://www.veterans-uk.info/ contains information on how to access service records post-1920.

Taxation Records

Until the seventeenth century taxation was regarded as an extraordinary source of revenue levied for specific purposes such as the defence of the realm, the king's marriage or the knighting of his eldest son. Originally taxation fell on land and property with the barons, the burghs and the church sharing the burden. Various early attempts at taxation can be found in taxation records in the Exchequer records (NAS ref. E59– 70).

Hearth tax, 1691–1695
In 1690 Parliament granted a tax of 14 shillings on every hearth in the kingdom payable by both landowners and tenants to raise money for the army. Only hospitals and the poor living on charity from the parish were exempt. There were huge difficulties in collecting the tax, particularly in highland or remote areas.

There records are held by the NAS (NAS ref. E69) and vary in quality of the information provided. The records are generally arranged by county and parish and may give the number of hearths in the parish, the names of the occupiers or owners of the houses and the number and names of exempt poor. However some lists, such as those for parishes in Glasgow, give only the total number of hearths and money collected, while those for

Inverness-shire give the total number of hearths headed by the name of the heritor and the names of the individual poor.

Many lists have not survived. There are none for any of the Orkney and Caithness parishes. Some hearth books were never handed in to the Exchequer and a few survive among collections of private papers. The Leven and Melville papers (NAS ref. GD26/7/300–391) contain lists for parishes in Dumfriesshire, Fife, Edinburgh, and Shetland. Lists for parishes in Ross-shire are in the Cromartie papers (NAS ref. GD305/1/164).

Poll tax, 1693–1699

Poll taxes were imposed in 1694, 1695 and twice in 1698 to pay off the debts and arrears of the army and navy. Payment was graduated at the rate of 6 shillings and upwards according to rank and means; only the poor and children under 16 were exempt. The collectors of the poll tax faced similar difficulties to those of the hearth tax and the records are incomplete. Arranged by county and parish, the amount of information provided varies from list to list (NAS ref E70). Some lists name children and servants.

Eighteenth-century taxation

After 1748 certain assessed taxes were levied in Scotland and lists of those assessed to pay them survive in the Exchequer records. The Window, Commutation, Inhabited House and Consolidated Assessed Taxes were all taxes on householders though in practice only the better off were taxed. The house had to have at least 7 windows or a rent of at least £5 to be taxed. The war with France from 1793 onwards resulted in the extension of taxation to other forms of property and imposed additional duties on those already taxed. The records of each tax are organised by county and parish with royal burghs listed separately. (NAS ref. E326)

Midlothian tax records 1735–1820

The Midlothian tax records are the working records of the Edinburgh county tax office. The records include land tax collection books, 1735–1803; income tax assessments, 1799–1801, property tax assessments, 1803–12; small house duty collections books, 1803–12; militia and reserve army, deficiency assessments, 1805; cash books and ledgers for payments to militia wives and families, 1803–15. (NAS ref. E327)

174

Death duties

Estate duty records relating to the various taxes levied on the estates of deceased persons are commonly known as death duties and are part of the records of the Inland Revenue in Scotland. These records begin in 1804. There is a closure period of 75 years on the modern records. The various registers and indexes provide information such as the relationship of beneficiaries to the deceased, date of death, names of executors and lawyers. (NAS ref. IRS5–14)

Business Records

Business records are an underused source for family historians. There are a number of collections in the NAS concerned with business records and overseas trade and many others are held at council and university archives. It is worthwhile searching the online catalogues for the NAS, the NRA and of local archives and libraries under either the name of the family (if they owned the business) or under the type of business. Records may include ledgers, journals, letter books, accounts, reports and correspondence. It is also worthwhile searching the NLS online catalogue for books on the particular trade in which your ancestor was involved.

Apprenticeships

Admission to one of the crafts or trades which were usually found within the Burghs was by serving an apprenticeship (an indenture), as son or son-in-law of a craftsman or for good services to the community. The Scottish Record Society has printed and indexed the registers of apprentices for Edinburgh, covering the period 1585–1800. These volumes are available in most larger libraries and family history centres in Scotland. There is also a series of indentures covering the years 1695–1934 in the NAS (Reference RH9/17/274–326) although these are not indexed.

Tradespeople

Many people were not members of a craft, but carried out a trade such as shoemaking or weaving, often in combination with farming. Some directories for towns and cities give names of merchants and tradespeople going back to the second half of the eighteenth century. Nineteenth century post office directions also exist for a number of large towns and have sections covering trades, individuals and lists of those living in each street.

The books also include contemporary advertisements, which provide useful information in many of the local businesses. These can be found in local libraries and archives.

Businesses

Scotland has had its own registration system for limited companies since 1856. Most are held by the Registrar of Companies at 102 George Street, Edinburgh, but a list of all registered companies is at NAS with files of some dissolved companies.

Files of dissolved companies are held in the NSA under reference BT.2 in which series each company is listed by its number in the Register of Companies (BT.1). The BT.2 company records consist of memoranda of association, lists of directors and shareholders (with addresses and occupation) financial statements and details of the winding up.

If the business was involved in litigation, then search the court records. If the company went bankrupt, then there should be information in the Court of Sessions records and possibly sheriff court records too.

The NAS also holds an extensive collection of business records. A useful guide can be found in J Imrie, 'National archive sources for business history' in *Studies in Scottish business history*, edited by P L Payne (London, 1967). Also useful is the *Dictionary of Scottish business biography, 1860 – 1960*, edited by Anthony Slaven and Sydney Checkland in two volumes covering the staple industries and the processing, distribution and service industries (Aberdeen, 1986 and 1990).

The following list gives selected collection titles and covering dates for records held in the NAS. These can be consulted at the search room in West Register House. However, as many are out-housed and will need to be brought in to the search room, you should contact the NAS in advance of your visit to avoid delays.

Description	NAS reference	Dates
Baillie Gifford & Co, investment managers, including Abbots Investment Trust	GD378	1909–1986
Balfour Group, chemical engineers, Leven	GD410	1834–1976
James Bertram & Son Ltd, papermill owners, Leith	GD284	1847–1972
Bertrams (Sciennes) Ltd, paper machinery manufacturer	GD419	1821–1980

BP Oil UK Ltd	GD454	1688–1970
British Bakeries (Scotland) Ltd	GD414	1894–1955
Caledonian Insurance Company	GD294	1805–1939
Canonmills cooperage, Edinburgh	GD287	1862–1970
Carron Company	GD58	1478–1982
A and T Constable, printers, Edinburgh	GD222	1878–1944
James Currie and Co, rag, bone and scrap merchants, Dundee	GD1/563	1874–1889
Dobie and Son, painters and Decorators, Edinburgh	GD1/1190	1849–1987
Dobbie McInnes Ltd, instrument makers	GD1/780	1893–1972
Granton Harbour Ltd, Edinburgh	GD290	1841–1967
Hawthorn Leslie (Engineers) Ltd	GD369	1863–1959
Inveresk Paper Company	GD269	1876–1965
Invergarry Iron Works	GD1/168	1726–1838
Leith Dock Commission	GD229	1799–1967
Lochleven Shipping Co Ltd	GD447	1907–1917
Morton of Darvel, textiles	GD236	1873–1978
Muirkirk Iron Company, in the Seaforth Muniments	GD46	
Palace and Playhouse Cinemas, Edinburgh	GD289	1927–1973
New Zealand and Australian Land Co.	GD435	1862–1963
Parsons Peebles Ltd, motor and generator manufacturers	GD349	1900–1978
Sandeman & Sons Ltd, wine and spirit merchants	GD408	1860–1914
Scottish Agricultural Industries Ltd	GD270	1837–1957
Sun Alliance	GD354	1775–1921
United Biscuits, including the records of Macfarlane Lang & Co and McVitie & Price	GD381	1878–1980
Victoria Rubber Co Ltd	GD404	1876–1979
Wright and Jobson Ltd, yarn spinners, Galashiels	GD1/852	1882–1976

The NAS also holds records of the Upper Clyde Shipbuilders (UCS) and other shipbulding companies on the upper and lower Clyde, from the Ayrshire Coast and from the Estuaries of the Forth and Tay. Though the collections include a little eighteenth century material, the bulk dates from the late nineteenth and twentieth centuries.

The records of the former coal companies held by the NSA include wages books, account books and sales books for individual collieries. The earliest record is of Lothian Coal Company in 1752 (CB.9), but most of the records are nineteenth and twentieth century.

Hudson Bay Company

For many centuries many Scots worked for the Hudson Bay Company which traded in northern and western Canada exporting animal skins to Europe and importing goods for sale to the native peoples. The Company was founded in 1670 and for nearly three centuries its headquarters was in London. It was transferred to Winnipeg in the late 1960s along with its archives. As a condition of allowing the export of its records, the company provided the National Archives in London with a microfilm copy, which is held in series BH 1. The website of the Provincial Archives of Manitoba, which holds the original material, is http://www.gov.mb.ca/chc/archives/hbca.

THE ARCHIVES

General Register Office of Scotland

The GROS holds Scottish statutory registers of births, deaths and marriages from 1855 onwards, census returns, 1841–1901, parish registers for the whole of Scotland and various other collections. For details of their holdings see www.gro-scotland.gov.uk

National Archives of Scotland

The NAS (also known as General Register House and formerly known as the Scottish Record Office) is the repository of records relating to the government and legal system of Scotland. It also holds church records, wills and testamentary records, private collections including landed estate records and business records.

The NAS has two search rooms, one at the east end of Princes Street (next to New Register House) and the other at West Register House in Charlotte Square. Most court records and a very large collection of maps and plans are kept at West Register House. The NAS website gives access to a number of fact sheets which will be of interest to the family historian. For details of their holdings see http://www.nas.gov.uk/

In the late 1990s the NAS became a pioneer in the digitisation and provision of online access to historical records on a very large scale, under the auspices of the Scottish Archive Network (SCAN) project, whose partners were the National Archives of Scotland (NAS), the Heritage Lottery Fund (HLF), and the Genealogical Society of Utah (now Family Search). The SCAN project created a single electronic catalogue to the holdings of more than 50 Scottish archives. Consult the SCAN online catalogue www.scan.org.uk and click on the archive in which you are interested.

The National Library of Scotland

The NLS is situated on George IV Bridge, Edinburgh, and is a copyright library holding a vast number of books and periodicals and a large collection of manuscripts relating to Scottish history. Catalogues of both books and manuscripts are online at www.nls.ul.

Local Archives and Libraries

In 1996 Scotland's local government was reorganised and the country was divided into districts administered by thirty-two unitary authorities. Each of these districts should have an archivist. The NAS has returned some local records held by them, including burgh and kirk session records, to these local archives. The catalogues of many of their holdings are online. Consult the SCAN online catalogue www.scan.org.uk and click on the archive in which you are interested.

Public libraries in Scotland also hold some original material or copies of records held by the NAS see. www.familia.org.uk for details.

USEFUL ADDRESSES

General Register Office for Scotland
New Register House
3 West Street
Edinburgh EH1 3YT
0131 3340380
www.gro-scotland.gov.uk

National Archives of Scotland
H.M. General Register House
2 Princes Street
Edinburgh EH1 3YY
0131 5351314
http://www.nas.gov.uk/

National Library of Scotland
George IV Bridge
Edinburgh EH1 3YY
0131 5351314
www.nas.gov.uk

ScotlandsPeople Centre
New Register House
3 West Register Street
Edinburgh EH1 3YT
www.ScotlandsPeoplehub.gov.uk/

Regional Repositories

Aberdeen City Archives
(includes Kinross)
Dunbar Street
Aberdeen AB24 3UJ
01224 481775
www.aberdeenshire.gob.uk

Angus Archives
Hunter Library
Restenneth Priory
By Forfar DD8 2SZ
01307 468644
www.angus.gov.uk/history/archives

Argyll and Bute Archives
Kilmory
Manse Brae
Lochgilphead
Argyll PA31 8RT
01456 604774
www.argyll-bute.gob.uk

Argyll and Bute Library
Library Headquarters
Highland Avenue
Sandbank
Dunoon PA23 8PB
01369 703214
www.argyll-bute.gov.uk

Ayrshire Archives Centre
Craigie Estate
Ayr KA8 0SS
01292 287584
www.ayrshirearchives.org.uk

Clackmannanshire Archives
26–28 Drysdale Street
Alloa FK10 1JL
01259 722262

Clydesdale District Libraries
(includes Lanark)
Lindsay Institute
Hope Street
Lanark ML11 7NH
01555 661331
www.southlanarkshire.gov.uk

Dornoch Digital Archive
Dornoch Library
Carnegie Buildings
High Street
Dornoch
Sutherland IV25 3SH
0186 2811079
www.highland.gov.uk

Dumfries and Galloway Archives
(includes Kirkcudbright and
Wigtown)
Archive Centre
33 Burns Street
Dunfries DG1 2PS
01387 269254
www.dumgal.gov.uk/dumgal/
services.aspx?id=40

**Dumfries and Galloway Health
Board Archives**
Easterbrook Hall
Crichton Royal Hospital
Dumfries
DG1 4TG
01387 244228

Dundee City Archives
21 City Square
Dundee DD1 3BY
01382 434494
www.dundeecity.gov.uk/archive

**East Dunbartonshire Council
Information and Archives**
William Patrick Library
2–4 West High Street
Kirkintilloch G66 1AD
0141 7768090
www.eastdunbarton.gov.uk

**East Lothian Council Local History
Centre**
Haddington Library
Newton Port
Haddington EH41 3HA
01620 823307
www.eastlothian.gov.uk

Edinburgh City Archives
Department of Corporate Services
City of Edinburgh Council
City Chambers
High Street
Edinburgh EH1 1YJ
0131 5294616
www.edinburgh.gov.uk

Falkirk Council Archives
History research Centre
Callendar House
Callendar Park
Falkirk FK1 1YR
01324 503778
www.falkirk.gov.uk

Fife Council Archive Centre
Carleton House
The Haig Business Park
Balgonie Road
Markinch KY7 6AQ
01592 583352
www.fife.gov.uk

Glasgow Archives
Glasgow and City Archives and
District Libraries
Mitchell Library
North Street
Glasgow G3 7DN
0141 2272405
www.mitchelllirbary.org

Highland Council Archives
Inverness Libarary
Farraline Park
Inverness IV 1NH
01463 220330
www.highland.gov.uk

Moray Local Heritage Services
East End School
Institution Road
Elgin IV30 1RP
01343 569011
www.moray.gov.uk/localheritage

North Highland Archive
Wick Library
Sinclair Terrace
Caithnness KW1 SAB
01955 606432
www.highland.gov.uk

Orkney Library and Archive
44 Junction Road
Kirkwall
Orkney KW15 1AG
01856 873166
www.orkneylibrary.org.uk/html/
contact.htm

Perth and Kinross Council Archive
A.K. Bell Library
York Place
Perth PH2 SEP
01738 477012
www.pkc.gov.uk/archives

Scottish Borders Heritage Hub
Kirkstile
Hawick TD9 0AE
01450 360 699
www.scotborders.gov.uk/council/
specialinterest/heartofhawick

Shetland Islands Shetland
Museum and Archives
Hay's Dock
Lerwick
Shetland ZE1 0WP
01595 695057
www.shetlandmuseumandarchives.
org.uk

Stirling Council Archive Service
5 Borrowmeadow Road
Springkerse Industrial Estate
Stirling FK7 7UW
01786 450745
www.stirling.gov.uk/index/access-
info/archives.htm

West Lothian Council Archives and Records Management Centre
9 Dunlop Square
Deans Industrial Estate
Livingston EH54 8SB
01506 773770
www.westlothian.gov.uk/tourism/1488/archives/

Scottish Catholic Archives
Columba House,
16 Drummond Place,
Edinburgh EH3 6PL,
0131 556 3661
www.catholic-heritage.net

Scottish Jewish Archives Centre
Garnethill Synagogue
129 Hill Street
Glasgow G3 6UB
0141 3324911
www.sjac.org.uk

Family History Centres in Scotland

Aberdeen
North Anderson Drive
Aberdeen, Grampian, Scotland
0122 469 2206

Alloa
Grange Road
Westend Park
Alloa, Clackmannanshire, Scotland
0125 921 1148

Ayr
Corner of Orchard Ave &
Mossgiel Road
Ayr, Ayrshire, Scotland

Dumfries
36 Edinburgh Road
Albanybank, Dumfrieshire,
Scotland
0138 725 4865

Dundee
Bingham Terrace
Dundee, Tayside, Scotland
0138 245 1247

Edinburgh
30A Colinton Road
Edinburgh, Lothian, Scotland
0131 313 2762

Elgin
Pansport Road
Elgin, Morayshire, Scotland
0134 354 6429

Glasgow
35 Julian Avenue
Kelvinside
Glasgow, Glasgow, Scotland
0141 357 1024

Invergordon
Kilmonivaig Seafield
Portmahomack
Tain, Ross-shire, Scotland
0186 287 1631

Inverness
13 Ness Walk
Inverness, Inverness-shire, Scotland
0146 323 1220

Kirkcaldy
Winifred Crescent
Forth Park
Kirkcaldy, Fifeshire, Scotland
0159 264 0041

Lerwick
44 Prince Alfred Street
Lerwick, Shetland, Scotland
0159 569 5732

Montrose
Coronation Way
Montrose, Angus, Scotland
0167 467 5753

Motherwell
444–478 Orbiston Street
Motherwell, Lanarkshire, Scotland
01698 266630

Paisley
Glenburn Road
Paisley, Renfrewshire, Scotland
0141 884 2780

Stornoway
Newton Street
Stornoway, Isle of Lewis, Scotland
0185 187 0972

SELECT BIBLIOGRAPHY

History

R D Anderson. *Education and the Scottish People, 1750–1918*. Oxford University Press. 1995.

Major R Money Barnes, *The Uniform and History of the Scottish Regiments*.

A D M Barrell. *Medieval Scotland*. Cambridge University Press. 2000. 296pp.

G W S Barrow. *Kingship and Unity: Scotland, 1000–1306*. Edinburgh University Press. 1989. 185pp.

Margaret Bennett, *Scottish Customs from the Cradle to the Grave*.

Christopher J. Berry. *Social Theory of the Scottish Enlightenment*. Edinburgh University Press. 1997.

Caroline Bingham. *The Stewart Kingdom of Scotland, 1371–1603*. Weidenfeld and Nicolson. 1974.

Jack Brand. *The National Movement in Scotland*. Routledge. 1978.

Callum G Brown. *Religion and Society in Scotland Since 1707*. Edinburgh University Press. 1997.

H M Chadwick. *Early Scotland: The Picts, the Scots & the Welsh of Southern Scotland*. Cambridge University Press. 1949.

David Daiches. *Scotland and the Union*. John Murray. 1977.

Neil Davidson. *The Origins of Scottish Nationhood*. Pluto Press. 2000.

T M Devine; Richard J. Finlay (editor*). Scotland in the Twentieth Century*. Edinburgh University Press. 1996. 312pp.

T M Devine, *The Scottish Nation 1700 to 2007* (rev ed. 2006)

T M Devine, *Scotland's Empire, 1600–1815*, Penguin Books. 2003.

T M Devine *The Transformation of Rural Scotland: social change and the agrarian economy, 1660–1815*, 1994.

T M Devine *Conflict and Stability in Scottish Society, 1700–1850* (Editor), 1990.

T M Devine, *The Great Highland Famine*, 1988.

Robert A. Dodgshon. *Land and Society in Early Scotland*. Clarendon Press. 1981.

Gordon Donaldson. *Scotland: The Shaping of a Nation*. David & Charles. 1974.

F D Dow. *Cromwellian Scotland, 1651–1660*. Edinburgh: John Donald. 1979.

Andrew Drummond and James Bulloch, The Scottish Church, 1688–1843 (Edinburgh, 1973).

Andrew Drummond and James Bulloch, *The Church in Victorian Scotland, 1843–74* (Edinburgh, 1975).

William Ferguson. *The Identity of the Scottish Nation: An Historic Quest.* Edinburgh University Press. 1998.

William Ferguson. *Scotland: 1689 to the Present.* Praeger. 1968.

Sally Foster. *Picts, Gaels and Scots: Early Historic Scotland.* Sterling Publishing Company. 2004.. Updated edition.

Michael Fry, *The Scottish Empire*, Phantassie. 2001.

George Gordon (editor). *Perspectives of the Scottish City.* Aberdeen University Press. 1985.

Clare Jackson. *Restoration Scotland, 1660–1690: Royalist Politics, Religion and Ideas.* Boydell Press. 2003.

James G Kellas. *Modern Scotland: The Nation Since 1870.* Praeger. 1968.

William Knox. *Industrial Nation: Work, Culture and Society in Scotland, 1800–Present.* Edinburgh University Press. 1999.

Bruce Lenman. *An Economic History of Modern Scotland, 1660–1976.* Archon Books. 1977.

Michael Lynch. *Scotland: A New History.* Century. 1991.

Michael Lynch, (ed) *The Oxford Companion to Scottish History*, (Oxford, 2001)

Magnus Magnusson. *Scotland: The Story of a Nation.* Grove Press. 2003.

William Law Mathieson. *Scotland and the Union: A History of Scotland from 1695 to 1747.* Glasgow: James Maclehose and Sons. 1905.

Rosalind Mitchison. *A History of Scotland.* Routledge. 2002.. 3rd Edition.

John Prebble, *Culloden.* Atheneum. 1962.

John Prebble, *The Highland Clearances*, Secker & Warburg, 1963.

John Prebble, *Glencoe: The Story of the Massacre*, Secker & Warburg. 1966.

John Prebble, *The Lion in the North: A Personal View of Scotland's History.* Penguin Books. 1973.

John Prebble, *Darien: The Scottish Dream of Empire.* Penguin Books. 1968.

John Prebble, *Mutiny: Highland Regiments in Revolt.* Penguin Books. 1975.

John Prebble *The King's Jaunt: George IV in Scotland, August, 1822*, Birlinn Limited. Edinburgh. 1988.

George Smith Pryde, *The Burghs of Scotland*, (Glasgow, 1965).

R L Graeme Ritchie. *The Normans in Scotland.* Edinburgh University Press. 1954.

James Scotland, *History of Scottish Education*, (London, 1969).

George Seaton, *Sketch of the history and imperfect condition of the parochial records in Scotland*, (Edinburgh, 1854).

T C Smout. *A History of the Scottish People, 1560–1830.* (London, 1969).

T C Smout, *A History of the Scottish People, 1830–1950*, (London, 1986).

David Turnock. *The Historical Geography of Scotland Since 1707: Geographical Aspects of Modernisation.* Cambridge University Press. 2005.
Christopher A. Whatley. *The Industrial Revolution in Scotland.* Cambridge University Press. 1997. 107pp. For the Economic History Society.
Jenny Wormald (editor). *Scotland: A History.* Oxford University Press. 2005.
Jenny Wormald. *Court, Kirk, and Community: Scotland, 1470–1625.* Edinburgh University Press. 1991.

Genealogy

Anthony Adolph, *Tracing Your Scottish Family History,* (Collins, 2008).
Robert Bain, *The Clans and Tartans of Scotland,* (Collins, 1968).
A R Bigwood, *Tracing Scottish Ancestors:* (Collins, 2001).
Rosemary Bigwood, *The Scottish Family Tree Detective,* (Manchester University Press, (2006).
George F Black, *The Surnames of Scotland:* (1996).
Kathleen B Cory, Leslie Hodgson, *Tracing Your Scottish Ancestry* (May 2004).
David Dorward, *Scottish Surnames,* (Collins, 1995).
Simon Fowler, *Tracing Your Scottish Ancestors* (Pocket Guides to Family History): (February 2001).
Graham S Holton, Jack Winch, *Discover Your Scottish Ancestry, Internet and Traditional Resources* (July 2003).
Sherry Irvine, *Your Scottish Ancestry, A Guide for North Americans* (November 1996).
Alwyn James, *Scottish Roots, a Step-By-Step Guide for Ancestor-Hunters in Scotland and Elsewhere* (April 1982). Roddy Martine, Don Pottinger, *Scottish Clan and Family Names, Their Arms, Origins and Tartans* (April 1992).
David Moody, *Scottish Family History,* (London, 1988).
David Moody, *Scottish Towns: Sources for Local Historians,* (London, 1992).
Judith P Reid, *Family Ties In England, Scotland, Wales, & Ireland: Sources for Genealogical Research* (June, 2002).
Cecil Sinclair *Tracing Scottish Local History* (HMSO 1994).
Margaret Stuart *Scottish Family History,* (Baltimore, 1978).
George Way of Plean and Romilly Squire, *Clans and Tartans,* (Collins, 1995).
Donald Whyte, *Scottish Surnames:* (May 2000).

INDEX